LEGENDARY RACING
MOTORCYCLES

LEGENDARY RACING
MOTORCYCLES

Mick Duckworth & Alan Seeley

Abbeydale Press

First published in 2007 by Abbeydale Press.
An imprint of Bookmart Limited.

Trading as Bookmart Limited
Blaby Road, Wigston
Leicestershire LE18 4SE
England

© 2007 Bookmart Limited

ISBN: 978-186147-206-9
Registered Number 2372865

Produced for Bookmart Limited by:
Editorial Developments,
Edgmond, Shropshire,
England

Design by: Bacroom Design and Advertising, Birmingham, England
Index: Marie Lorimer Indexing Services, Harrogate, England

Printed in China

CONTENTS

6 .... **Foreword**

7 .... **Introduction**

10 .... **AJS** 1954 7R3

14 .... **Britten** 1000cc

18 .... **BSA** 1970 750cc

22 .... **Ducati** .... 1979 900cc NCR

26 .... **Ducati** 1994 916

30 .... **Ducati** .... 2006 999 WSB

34 .... **Harley-Davidson** .... 1970 XR 750 TT

38 .... **Harley-Davidson** .... 1980 XR 750

42 .... **Honda** 1960s RC174

46 .... **Honda** 1960s RC162

50 .... **Honda** 1983 NS500

54 .... **Honda** 1980s VFR750/RC30

58 .... **Honda** 1991 RS125

62 .... **Honda** .... 2006 Repsol RC211V

66 .... **Kawasaki** 1975 H1-R

70 .... **Kawasaki** .... 1975 KR 750

74 .... **Kawasaki** 1980-1981 KR250

78 .... **Laverda** 1978 V6

82 .... **Moto Guzzi** 1957 V8

86 .... **MV** .... 1972 Agusta 750cc

90 .... **MV** .... 1973-1974 Agusta 500cc

94 .... **Norton** .... 1972 750cc John Player, TX72

98 .... **Norton** .... 1973 750cc John Player, Monocoque

102 .... **Norton** .... 1992 NRS588 Rotary

106 .... **Rea Yamaha** 1977 750cc

110 .... **Suzuki** 1980 XR34/RGC500

114 .... **Suzuki** 1979 XR23B/RGB700

118 .... **Suzuki** 1981 XR69/GS1000R

122 .... **Suzuki** 1984 XR45

126 .... **Suzuki** .... 1998 GSX-R 750 WSB

130 .... **Triumph** .... 1970-1975 750cc T150 Trident

134 .... **Triumph** .... 1971 750cc triple

138 .... **Yamaha** 1975 TZ750

142 .... **Yamaha** 1976 TZ250

146 .... **Yamaha** 1981 YZR500/OW53

150 .... **Yamaha** 2004 YZR/M1

154 .... **Stats**

158 .... **Index**

160 .... **Acknowledgements**

Foreword

When I was approached to write a foreword to this book "LEGENDARY RACING MOTORCYCLES" I casually glanced through the list of bikes that had been selected and classified as legendary. The 'Collins Concise Dictionary' says Legendary means as part 'very famous or notorious'. The authors, Mick Duckworth and Alan Seeley, with so many motorcycles to choose from, spanning over so many years, have included in their selection, great examples of racing machines that can be classed as either famous, notorious or both.

Having this book in my library will provide a fabulous historical reference both visually and technically long after the memories of the mind have faded into the distant past.

Each bike featured has played an important part in motorcycling history and of these machines featured I have been extremely lucky enough to race the Kawasaki KR750, the Suzuki XR69, XR34 and XR23 all with notable success.

However my choice personally would have to be the 1981 XR69. It was not only a bullet-proof missile but it took me to two TT victories and numerous race wins, including the British TTF1 Championship. When I arrived on the grid aboard my GS1000R XR69, other riders would look at me from under their visors with a look that told me I had 3 testicles, when they knew they only had two. I had them beaten from the start with the sheer grunt, exemplary handling and that stunning Texaco Heron Suzuki GB paint livery. Long live the GS1000 XR69.

Enjoy the read

Introduction

Motorcycle racing is surely the most thrilling and absorbing of all motorised sports. Who can fail to be excited by the noise of revving engines, the smell of spent oil and riders dicing at insane speeds with only tiny patches of tyre rubber to keep them from disaster?

It takes talent, physical fitness, mental fortitude – and some luck - to join the world's bike racing elite. But however good a rider is, he or she will need the best hardware for anything more than flash-in-the-pan success. Having the most powerful engine helps, but it's rarely enough. Controllability, agility, aerodynamics and braking can be just as important.

The rival teams are constantly striving to create a better machine and achieve ever-faster lap times. Winning not only gains prestige for the manufacturer, it hastens technical progress and boosts the sales of showroom machines. This has been the case since the first circuit races were held early in the last century and the story of the endless drive for improvement with its pay-offs, breakthroughs and occasional blind alleys is fascinating.

The Legendary Bikes featured on the following pages show how over the decades designers, engineers and other technicians have endeavoured to shape winners while working within rules that dictate engine capacity, machine dimensions and the type of fuel allowed.

Some are the purest of racers, designed specifically for grand prix events and often produced at vast expense to the factories involved. Of those many have two-stroke power, which came into its own from the Sixties, when sophisticated induction and exhaust timings were perfected to obtain power outputs that a four-stroke engine of the same capacity could not match. In time, however, the high-performance two-stroke, with its prodigious thirst for fuel and exhaust emissions, gave way to machinery more closely related to products that manufacturers sell to the public.

There are no-holds-barred four-strokes here, too, like Moto Guzzi's astonishing V8 of the Fifties, Honda's miniaturised marvels of the Sixties and the MV Agusta that made the last stand for four-strokes in the 500cc world championship, once the premier class in grand prix racing. You'll also find the extraordinary hand-built Britten V-twin and the Yamaha M1 raced by the great Valentino Rossi in Moto GP.

Then there are racers built to a formula that requires them to be based on a production model. In theory this type of racing puts everyone on equal terms, but works-prepared machines for top riders usually have the edge, thanks to special kit. Examples are the factory versions of Yamaha's Formula 750 bike and the Honda RC30 for the Superbike category.

For good measure, we've also thrown in something completely different: a Harley-Davidson V-twin built for the peculiarly American form of dirt oval track racing.

This book is not just about machinery, for every successful racing campaign ultimately depends on the rider. Some of the best are just plain fearless while others are a key part of the development process: all are exceptional characters.

Read on and enjoy!

AJS 7R3 1954 350cc

When the British AJS factory wheeled out its 7R3 in 1952, some people were baffled by its design. The 7R3's 350cc single-cylinder engine had three valves: one inlet and two for exhaust. Surely, they thought, it should be the other way round to achieve efficient combustion chamber filling and gain power?

But the engine's designer H J Hatch had his reasons. A veteran engineer who had created the unorthodox four-valve Excelsior 'mechanical marvel' single that won the 1933 Lightweight TT, he was hired by AJS to revive the marque's flagging fortunes in GP racing.

Hatch's design was based on the existing AJS 7R single sold as a competitive three-fifty for privateers. Although the bottom-end was strengthened, he concentrated his radical changes on the upper engine.

Using the materials available at the time, the fastest machines suffered excessive heat build-up in long races and exhaust valve failures were often the result. Hatch's solution was to have two small valves. The heat path from their centres to the seats was shorter, while doubled-up seats and valve guides would transfer heat to the cylinder head metal effectively.

The spark plug's central location aided efficient combustion and the splayed exhaust ports exposed the central portion of the cylinder head to a blast of cooling air. A cool-running head boosts power and maintains it during a long race.

Rather than the 7R's single camshaft, Hatch's 'triple knocker' layout used a transverse shaft to open the inlet valve and two longitudinal camshafts for the exhausts.

One of the AJS three-valver's last race appearances. Scots rider Bob McIntyre eases the clutch to change gear during the 350cc Scarborough International Gold Cup race in 1954. He finished second to John Surtees' MV Agusta four. It was AJS company policy to race without fairings, but this would make little difference on Scarborough's short and twisty Oliver's Mount circuit.

While the new engine did not win races in 1952, it gained several podium places including New Zealander Rod Coleman's third in the 350cc Junior TT. And its durability was proved by world records set at the Montlhèry banked circuit in France, one being gained by averaging 98.62mph (158.71km/h) for seven hours. In 1953 Coleman led the 350cc TT for two laps before the valve gear failed, due, the rider said, to his being under-geared.

In 1954, the AJS team's new chief Jack Williams boosted the engine's output and improved the machine's aerodynamics. Astonishingly, it was against company policy to fit fairings, which were commonplace in GP racing by the mid-Fifties. However Williams lowered the whole cycle and used a deep fuel tank surrounding the upper engine. A fuel pump fed the carburettor, and cool air was led to it by intakes in the tank sides.

The new-look 7R3 won in the 1954 TT, with Coleman finishing ahead of similarly mounted team-mate Derek Farrant. Reliability won the day after Moto Guzzis that held an early lead retired and Norton rider Ray Amm, who pushed the lap record beyond 94mph, also dropped out.

H J Hatch died in 1954 and his creation was shelved when AJS failed to field a works team for 1955. In any case, the 7R3 would have been outpaced by lightweight streamlined Guzzis, which dominated the 350cc class that season. But the triple knocker's TT victory and the world speed records stand as proof of its reliability.

Specifications

Make/Model: *AJS 7R3*

Engine type:
Air-cooled, single cylinder tohc four-stroke
Displacement: *349cc (75.5 x 78mm)*
Fuel system: *1 3/16in Amal TT mm carburettor*
Lubrication system: *dry sump*
Maximum power: *41ps @ 7,800rpm*
Maximum speed: *120mph/193km/h*

Transmission:
Gearbox: *4-speed*
Primary drive: *chain*
Clutch: *dry, multi-plate*
Final drive: *chain*

Chassis and Running Gear:
Frame type: *tubular double cradle*
Front suspension: *telescopic fork*
Rear suspension: *swingarm with twin shocks*
Front/rear wheels: *wire spoked 19in*
Front/rear tyres: *Dunlop Racing*
Front brake: *8in twin-leading-shoe drum*
Rear brake: *8in drum*
Weight: *not available*
Fuel capacity: *28 litres*

Lowered and streamlined for 1954, the 7R3 has a pannier-style fuel tank of a type AJS also used on its 500cc E95 twin. The man behind the remodelling was Jack Williams, father of Peter Williams, who designed pannier-tanked Nortons in the Seventies.

Hidden engine has three overhead camshafts, operating one inlet valve and two small splayed exhaust valves. The handlebars are an early form of the clip-on type, fixed directly to the front fork tubes.

Owned by the National Motorcycle Museum, this surviving
1954 machine was restored by Team Obsolete in the USA.

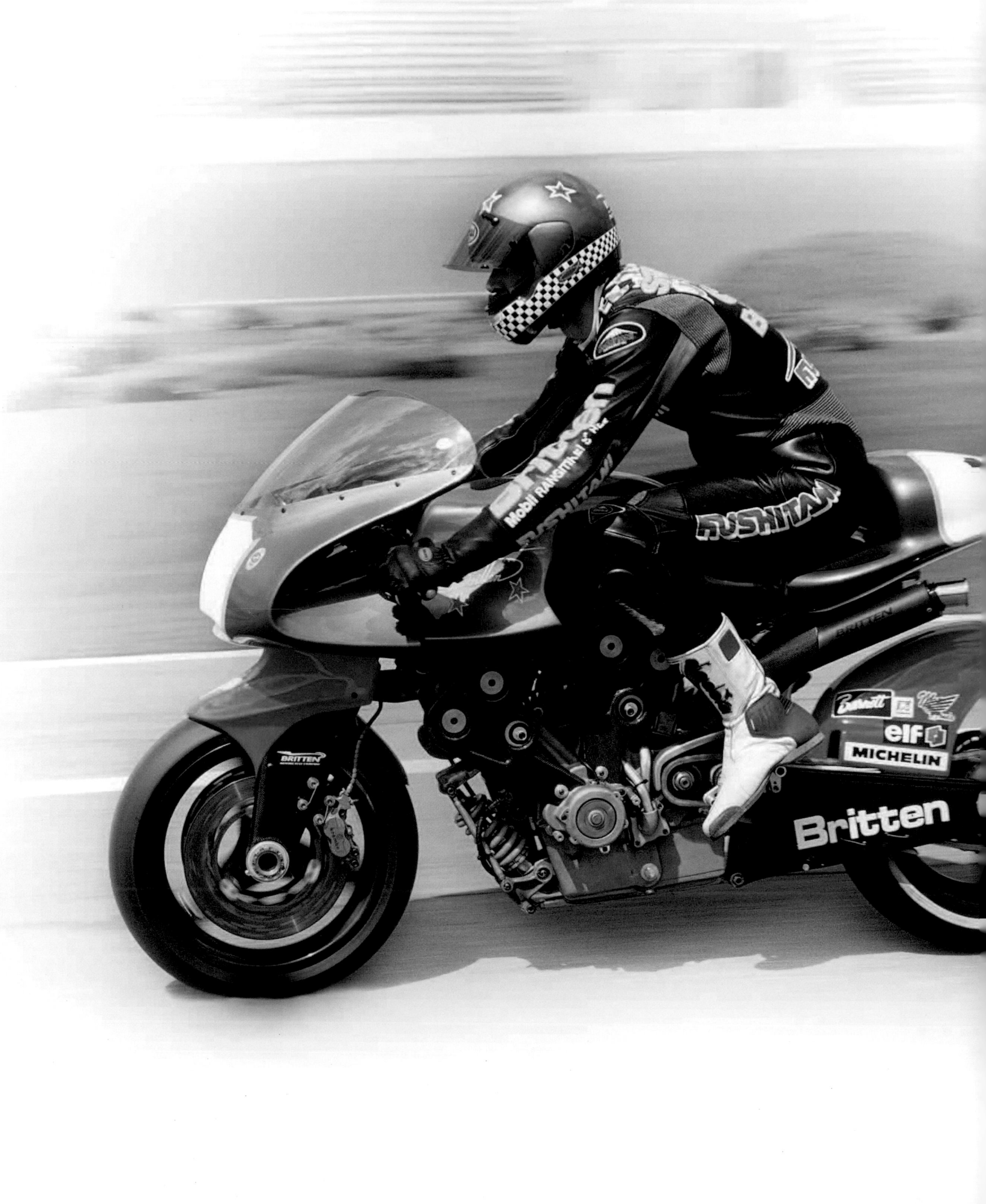
BRITTEN
elf
MICHELIN
Britten

Britten V1000

John Britten was a staggering individual. Even in a sport like motorcycle racing filled with single-minded geniuses, Britten stood out. A New Zealand mechanical engineer, sometime racer, property developer and lighting manufacturer, Britten decided to build and develop his own V-twin racer, engine and all, following frustrating experiments with a Ducati race bike and a Denco engine in a home-made frame. He would eventually produce a giant-slayer in the form of the V1000, a bike that would enjoy much Battle of the Twins and BEARS success (BEARS stands for British European and American Racing – no one knows whether the 'S' stands for 'supporters' or 'society'), and in the hands of another Kiwi, Andrew Stroud would win the inaugural International BEARS Championship, with his team-mate Steven Harris runner-up. This success was especially poignant as it came at a time when Britten was in the last stages of terminal cancer.

The Britten is an amazingly singular bike. Front forks are made of carbon-fibre and revived and updated a girder fork theory that had last been seen on an English Vincent of the seventies. Bodywork was protoyped using chicken wire, clay, and a hot-glue gun.

It was a hard and difficult road to race success for the Britten team, essentially a DIY operation up against the might of the world's greatest race teams with their huge R&D budget. But a mixture of ingenuity, enthusiasm, energy and perseverance allowed Britten and the small dedicated team he assembled around him to prevail.

At its Daytona debut in 1989 the bike broke down at the first corner. The following year a cracked exhaust brought an impressive performance to an end. In 1991 the Britten showed its true potential with a second and a third in the Battle of the Twins. Then in 1994, Britten's Daytona dream finally came true with a win in what was by then called the Pro Twins race. At that point the bike was closer to 1100cc as the regulations allowed, but the company was by then building sub-litre versions of the bike to meet with regs for other race classes.

Andrew Stroud is the rider many race fans most closely associate with the Britten. Here he is carrying the number one plate earned by winning the first BEARS series. Stroud enjoyed much success on the Britten but perhaps his most celebrated victory was his giant-slaying win at the Pro Twins race at Daytona in 1994.

Of course the ultimate test for any race bike is the Isle of Man TT. Britten had entered Shaun Harris in the 1993 Senior and frustratingly, with fourth place or better in sight, the Britten lost its oil and was forced to retire,

The following year, Britten signed Irishman Mark Farmer and Yorkshire roads perennial Nick Jefferies. As a warm up for the TT they competed at the NW200 in Ulster where Jefferies was seventh while Farmer retired due to hydraulic lock after a mechanic had replaced oil-line banjoes with the wrong type. A third rider was to contest the TT, Robert Holden. But he decided not to ride the Britten and was replaced by another Kiwi, Jason McEwen, who ultimately was not allowed to start because of inadequate practice time. In the Formula One TT Jefferies retired with waterlogged ignition and retired in the Senior with a gearbox failure. Tragically, Mark Farmer crashed and died in practice.

Britten also took some FIM world records in 1993, the bike being ridden by teamster Loren Poole who rode a Britten to 188mph in NZ.

In a fitting postscript, Harris returned to the TT in 1996, the year after Britten's death, and finished 33rd in the Senior at a race average of 107.26mph.

To date only ten bikes have been built.

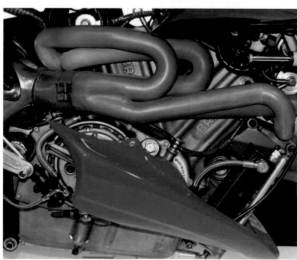

Specifications

Make/Model: Britten V1000

Engine type:
Liquid-cooled, 60-degree V-twin four-stroke.
Displacement: 985cc (99 x 64mm)
Fuel system: sequential fuel injection, two injectors per cylinder
Ignition: Programmable engine management computer with history facility
Lubrication system: wet sump
Maximum power: 166bhp @ 11,800rpm
Maximum speed: 188mph

Transmission:
Gearbox: 5-speed (optional 6-speed)
Primary drive: gears
Clutch: dry, multi-plate slipper clutch
Final drive: chain

Chassis and Running Gear:
Frame type: engine as stressed member
Front suspension: double wishbones with girder
Rear suspension: swingarm with Ohlins monoshock
Front/rear wheels: 17in Britten carbon composite
Front/rear tyres: Michelin
Front brake: 2 x 320mm discs
Rear brake: 210mm disc
Weight: 138kg (dry)
Fuel capacity: 24 litres

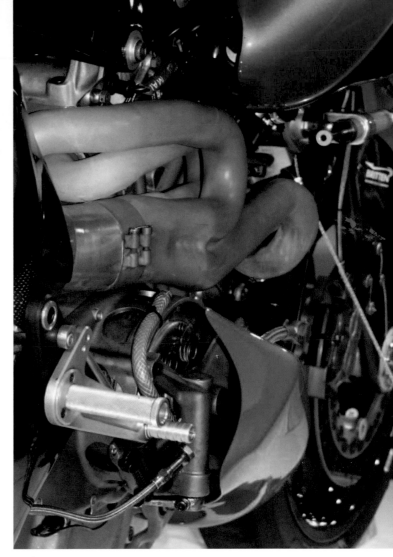

The Britten bristles with innovation and exotic material. Carbon fibre cambelt covers proudly bear the legend 'Made in New Zealand'. At the bottom left of the picture above, the shock absorber that controls the front wishbone suspension. Convoluted header pipes (right) are a labour-intensive work-of-art and are shaped as they are to provide the correct tuned length for the exhaust while allowing the silencer to be close to the middle of the bike for good mass centralisation.

This is bike number eight from ten built owned by the sensational Barber Museum in the United States. It was campaigned by the Barber race teams but suffered reliability issues, a common theme in the Britten history. While incredible performance made for some amazing achievements, ultimately it proved unreliable. Sent back to New Zealand for some expensive upgrades it still failed to perform reliably and now lives as a museum piece. Visitors love and worship it.

BSA triple 1970 750cc

Qualifying for the 1970 Daytona 200 was held on the banked tri-oval used for car racing at the famous Florida track. The fastest machines were the new three-cylinder Triumphs and BSAs, led by rising American star Gene Romero. He howled around at 157.34mph on his Triumph and was unofficially clocked at 165mph in a speed trap. Second fastest was nine-times Grand Prix world champion Mike Hailwood, who had been temporarily lured away from car racing to join the BSA team in a massive British assault on the US racing scene.

A fleet of six triples had been built at the BSA Group-owned Triumph factory to comply with the road racing formula introduced in the USA for 1970. It admitted any roadster-based engine up to 750cc, which could be installed in full-race cycle parts provided they were generally available.

The British contenders were powered by ohv pushrod engines from the 750cc BSA Rocket 3 and Triumph Trident roadsters launched for 1969. The two units were almost identical, except that the Triumph had vertical cylinders while the BSA's were inclined forwards. The man overseeing preparation was Doug Hele, who had extensive experience of tuning Triumph's 500cc Daytona-winning twins and Norton Manx singles before that.

The triples' engine internals were lightened, and high-compression pistons used in conjunction with flowed combustion chambers, special cams, track carburettors and three-into-one exhausts. Coil ignition systems with contact breakers were powered by the existing crankshaft-mounted alternator.

The news that Honda had produced a 750cc four for the 1970 Daytona, sent the Triumph-BSA management into apoplexy. Bert Hopwood and Doug Hele had just three months to turn a heavy road bike into a slim race winner. Much depended on the results at Daytona and the BSA trump card was to hire Mike Hailwood, nine times World Champion. Although he didn't win, he led the race for 12 laps before a hole burnt in a piston. The badge engineered Triples went onto a successful career in the US and at home.

In pre-race qualifying tests at Daytona, the Hailwood BSA did 152.99mph - a shade faster than the winning Honda. Drum front brakes (below) were well ventilated, a requirement for the gruelling Daytona race.

Welding wizard Rob North was commissioned to fabricate double loop frames in T45 tubing. Selectively assembled roadster front forks were used with Italian Fontana drum brakes while rear braking was by lightweight discs. Aerodynamic fairings and seat tails, vital for the fast Daytona track, were developed in the Royal Aircraft Establishment's wind tunnel.

Ducting was devised to aid air cooling, but abandoned in Florida when it was found that hot air was boiling fuel in the carburettors' float chambers.

In the 200-mile race, on a circuit comprising part of the tri-oval banking plus a twisty infield section, BSA's number one rider Hailwood contested the lead with American Triumph teamster Gary Nixon in the early stages. But after only 12 laps, failing valve gear forced him out and mechanical trouble also sidelined Nixon.

Daytona veteran Dick Mann won the race for Honda on a special version of the CB750 Four roadster. Nursing an ailing engine, he came in ten seconds ahead of Romero, who lost time overshooting a bend early in the race. Another Triumph triple rider, Don Castro, was third.

Ex-BSA rider Mann was rapidly returned to the fold and he rode the Hailwood bike on the new Talladega track in Alabama in May 1970. Despite having American Bendix ignition points better able to cope with higher rpm than the Lucas originals, a misfire meant he could only manage fourth. However, the winner of the 200-mile event was another works BSA triple ridden by American David Aldana, whose average speed of 104.59mph (168.28km/h) was the highest ever seen in an American road race.

Specifications

Make/Model: BSA

Engine type:
Air-cooled, in-line, three-cylinder ohv four-stroke.
Displacement: 741cc (67 x 70mm)
Fuel system: 3 x 1 3/16in Amal GP carburettors
Lubrication system: dry sump
Maximum power: 84ps @ 7,500rpm
Maximum speed: 165mph/266 km/h

Transmission:
Gearbox: 5-speed
Primary drive: chain
Clutch: dry, single plate
Final drive: chain

Chassis and Running Gear:
Frame type: tubular, full loop, double cradle
Front suspension: telescopic fork
Rear suspension: tubular swingarm with twin Girling shocks
Front/rear wheels: wire spoked 19in
Front/rear tyres: Dunlop KR76 3.00 x 19in/KR73 3.50 x 19in
Front brake: 250mm Fontana double twin-leading shoe drum
Rear brake: 230mm disc with AP Lockheed caliper
Weight: 172kg (380 lb)
Fuel capacity: 25 litres

The fuel filler is positioned in a cut-out at the front of the seat, behind the fuel tank (above). An oil cooler can be seen just above the engine.

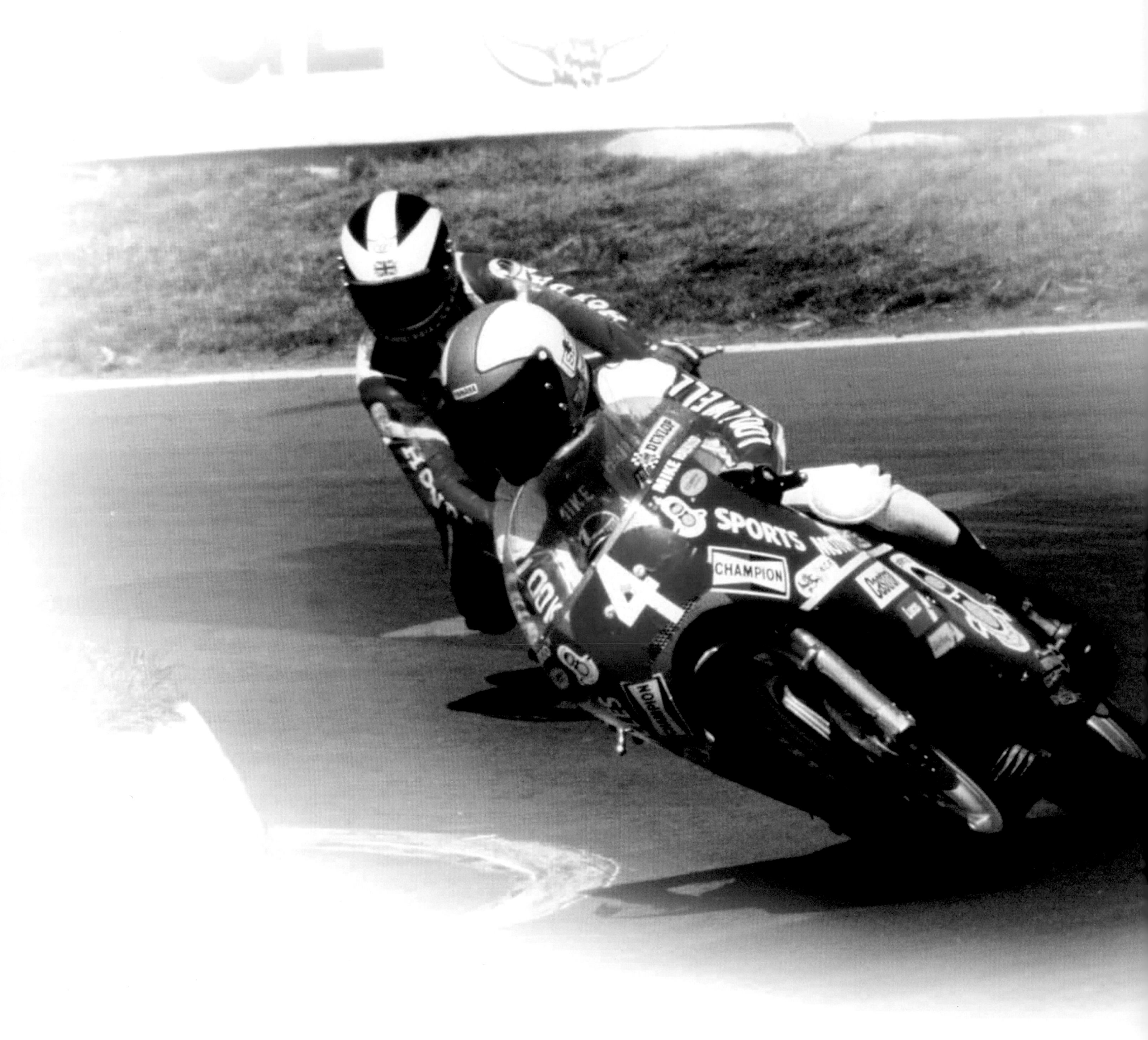
SPORTS
CHAMPION
DUNLOP
4

Ducati NCR 1979 900cc

It was motorcycle racing's perfect fairy tale. In 1978, retired nine-times world champion Mike Hailwood returned to the Isle of Man TT after 11 years' absence. Riding a dealer-funded Ducati V-twin, the 38-year-old roared to a popular win at record speed in the TT Formula One race, ahead of younger men on Japanese fours. His nearest rival Phil Read tried to keep up on an official Honda four, until it stopped with an oil leak.

The sure-steering 884cc Ducati had been prepared by Cheshire-based Sports Motor Cycles with assistance from the Italian factory. Built by NCR (Nepoti and Caracchi Racing), a Bologna equipe closely linked to Ducati, it was homologated as a derivative of Ducati's 900SS roadster. It was decked out in Sports Motor Cycles' red, white and green livery, based on Castrol oil packaging and coincidentally the colours of the Italian flag.

Ducati promised stronger support for the 1979 event, effectively fielding a factory team with Hailwood riding again and Steve Wynne of Sports Motor Cycles as team manager.

As things turned out, the 1978 fairy tale was too good to repeat. Hailwood fell off when testing one of the new twins in Italy and they weren't shipped until shortly before the TT, so Wynne could not spend much time on Island-focused preparation.

After practising on a 950cc bike intended for the open 1000cc TT Classic race, Mike was unhappy with its handling on the Mountain Course's twisty and bumpy roads. He opted instead to ride the two-stroke being provided by Suzuki GB for him to race in the 500cc Senior event.

Fresh from his 1978 Isle of Man Formula One victory, Mike Hailwood rubs it in by beating Phil Read's Honda four at the Mallory Park Post TT meeting. Mike's 1979 F1 machine, built to conform with tighter application of the rulebook, did not enjoy the same sparkling success.

Although built up as favourite in the Formula One race, the veteran struggled to stay among the leaders on Honda's latest 998cc 16-valve dohc fours. He probably had less power than in the previous year, because tightening of the TT Formula rules had forced Ducati to use an engine more closely based on the standard 900SS unit.

The dogged Hailwood rode as only he could, holding third place ahead of Honda's Ron Haslam for three of the six laps until the Ducati lost its top gear on the final circuit. Then the engine cut out on the Mountain descent. Mike thought he'd wrecked the motor by over-revving but it turned out that a loose battery had disconnected itself.

Mike was not technically minded, but acting on advice from trackside marshals he re-made the connection and wedged the battery firmly between the frame and rear mudguard. The engine started and he rode on over the final mile to finish fifth. His best lap had been at 109.45mph, compared with his record 110.62mph in the 1978 race, while Honda's winner Alex George lapped at 112.94mph.

It wasn't all bad news for Ducati. The 1979 TT Formula One bike provided the pattern for one of the factory's best-selling roadsters, the Mike Hailwood Replica. Originally intended as a strictly limited-edition product when released in 1979, the MHR remained in the company's range until 1986.

Italian kit: front fork is Marzocchi, hydraulic brakes are Brembo and wheels by Campagnolo.

Rear caliper support is integral with a sliding block on the swingarm used to tension the drive chain.

Ducati 916 1994

One marque is more synonymous than any other with Superbike racing, and that's Ducati. And few machines are more iconic than the 916, both on road and track. At a time when Grand Prix machinery was becoming ever more esoteric and removed from the machines available to road riders, Superbike was the fast-rising production-based class where the machines bore more than a passing resemblance to the bikes available to mere mortals. The 916's beautiful lines helped cement the V-twin's instant legend.

The 916 was the long-awaited replacement for the 888 that had dominated World Superbikes from 1990 to 1992. Honda's RC30 750cc V4 had won the first two championships in 1988 and 1989 and for 1994 they were to enter a full factory team running the RC30's replacement, the RC45. Ducati delayed the replacement of the 888 to take Honda head on. They expected they would need something special to beat the Yen-rich Japanese, even despite the 250cc capacity and 15kg weight advantage afforded to twins over the 740cc fours.

The Italians had another score to settle. Brit Carl Fogarty had won 11 races for Ducati in 1993, but the championship went to Kawasaki's Scott Russell who despite having only five wins had been more consistent than Foggy and had crashed less.

Design genius Massimo Tamburini headed the project and it was hailed as a sensation when revealed to the press in late 1993. The elegant bodywork was inspired by Ducati's Supermono racer, designed by the often maligned Pierre Terblanche. The engine was a refinement of the highly developed 926cc 888 engine with the stroke lengthened to 66mm for homologation purposes. Where the 916's standard bore was 94mm (the 926cc 888 had a 96mm bore and 64mm stroke), Ducati bored a handful of the first 916 race engines out to 96mm to give a capacity of 955cc.

There have been many legends in motorcycle racing, but this rider and this machine are up there with the best. This is Carl Fogarty, guiding his beautiful, all-conquering Ducati 916 to victory. This wasn't the first time and would certainly not be the last.

The bike's weight was pared to the 145kg minimum, helped by the use of such exotic components as titanium Pankl conrods.

Carl Fogarty's team-mate in Ducati Corse was Giancarlo Falappa, and the other works-spec 955s went to Davide Tardozzi's rider Fabrizio Pirovano, Jamie Whitham riding for the UK Moto Cinelli team and Troy Corser, who was riding in AMA Superbikes and would contest the occasional WSB round. Sadly Falappa's career was ended by injuries sustained while testing at the fourth round in Albacete.

When it came down to it, the Honda threat didn't really materialise and they didn't win a race all year although works rider Aaron Slight visited second and third places a few more times than team-mate Doug Polen.

Foggy looked like he might repeat the previous season's pattern early on when he and Kawasaki's Russell took a win apiece at the opening round at Donington. King Carl then fell off and broke his wrist in qualifying for the next round at Hockenheim. But once fully fit he added a further nine wins giving him ten victories to Russell's nine and that extra 25 points was the margin that separated Foggy from his arch rival at the top of the table.

The 916 took Fogarty to the World Superbike Championship four times - 1994, 1995, 1998 and 1999. In 1996 Troy Corser also took the championship with the 916 - a truly incredible machine!

Specifications

Make/Model: *Ducati 916*

Engine type:
Liquid-cooled, V-twin four-stroke.
Displacement: *955cc (96 x 66mm)*
Fuel system: *Magnetti Marelli fuel injection*
Ignition: *Electronic*
Lubrication system: *wet sump*
Maximum power: *150bhp @ 11,000rpm*
Maximum speed: *Over 188mph/300kph*

Transmission:
Gearbox: *6-speed*
Primary drive: *gear*
Clutch: *dry, multi-plate*
Final drive: *chain*

Chassis and Running Gear:
Frame type: *tubular steel trellis*
Front suspension: *46mm Ohlins upside-down telescopic fork fully adjustable*
Rear suspension: *single-sided swingarm with fully adjustable Ohlins monoshock*
Front/rear wheels: *17in/17in*
Front/rear tyres: *12/60 VR17/18/60 VR17*
Front/rear brake: *Twin disc, floating, 320mm/single disc, 200mm*
Weight: *145kg (dry)*
Fuel capacity: *N/A*

Fogarty's machine (top), now displayed at the Ducati museum in Bologna, Italy. A modified road version (bottom), also displayed at the museum.

Ducati 999 2006 WSB

Troy Bayliss couldn't have picked a better place to win the 2006 World Superbike Championship than Imola, just a stone's throw from the Italian birthplace of Ducati motorcycles, Bologna. This was his second time, having taken the WSBK championship back in 2001. In the penultimate round of the 2006 series, held at the Autodromo Enzo & Dino Ferrari in front of 86,000 spectators, the thirty-seven-year-old Australian took the crown with a fifth place in race one. In the second race of the day Bayliss held the lead from start to finish, taking his eleventh win of the year in this extraordinary season. Bayliss's triumph takes the number of Riders' titles won by Ducati in the production-based series to twelve.

Just one week after Bayliss had clinched a twelfth rider title for Ducati at Imola, the Italian manufacturer concluded a perfect season by wrapping up the Manufacturers' crown at the Magny-Cours circuit in France too.

The astonishing Ducati 999F06 is a refinement of the machine that conquered the World Championship in its introductory years back in 2003 and 2004. The culmination of refining and fine-tuning the already well-proven four-stroke L-head engine and tubular trellis frame has made this machine all-conquering in the hands of Bayliss. Testing this monster was started in November of 2005 at Valencia and continued through to the opening round of the 2006 season at Quatar. Improvements were focused on the use of a new Öhlins hydraulic system applied to the new 42mm pressurised TTX20 upside-down forks and the TTX36 rear shock absorber. The new shock absorber design also helped to lose some 600 grams in overall weight.

This is Troy Bayliss at full concentration. The 2001 World Superbike champion from Taree, Australia, returned to the category in 2006 after three years in MotoGP, and took his second title. The twelve wins he captured in 2006 are testimony to the incredible competitiveness of the Australian, and he lines up for the next two seasons with the Ducati Xerox Team.

With a bore and stroke of 104mm x 58.8mm, the Ducati 999 Testastretta, with its desmodromically controlled double overhead cam and four valves per cylinder engine, produces 194hp @ 12,500rpm. Revving close to 13,000rpm, its electronically managed ignition and injection system uses a Magneti Marelli Marvel4 ECU to deliver Shell V-Power RD0502 fuel to a single Magneti Marelli IWF1 injector per cylinder. From a simple switch control, the rider is able to select any one of three pre-programmed ignition maps as well as automatically restrict his speed upon pit-lane entry. In addition to engine management, the Marvel4 ECU also looks after the bike's data logging functions.

The 999F06's slender overall weight, coupled with its impressive 194hp, achieves straightline speeds in excess of 194mph (312km/h). Brembo stopping power is fitted and the machine has an option of two 320mm or two 290mm Brembo floating discs, gripped by radial calipers with four 34mm pistons at the front, and an option of 200mm or 218mm vented, floating discs gripped by optional calipers equipped with four 24mm or two 34mm pistons at the rear.

Who said race bikes had no relevance to what happens on the streets? The 2005 season saw Shell's partnership with Ducati do just that. Shell Advance Racing X 4T, available for all ultra-high-performance superbikes, is identical to the Shell Advance M1854 - the lubricant which saw Ducati Corse take six World Superbike Manufacturer Championships and four Riders' Titles.

Specifications

Make/Model: *Ducati 999 WSB 2006*

Engine type:
Testastretta 4-stroke L-twin 90°
Displacement: *999 cc*
Fuel system: *Magneti Marelli electronic injection system*
Lubrication system: *Gear oil pump with oil cooler*
Maximum power: *194hp @12500 rpm*
Maximum speed: *194mph/312km/h*

Transmission:
Gearbox: *6-speed*
Primary drive: *Straight cut gears*
Clutch: *dry, multi-plate clutch*
Final drive: *Regina chain Ï*

Chassis and Running Gear:
Frame type: *tubular steel trestle*
Front suspension: *42mm pressurised TTX20 upside-down Öhlins fork*
Rear suspension: *dual-side aluminium swingarm with Öhlins TTX36 shock absorber*
Front/rear wheels: *Brembo/Marchesini 3.50 x17/5.50 x 17*
Front/rear tyres: *Pirelli 120/75 R420 (16.5")/ Pirelli 190/65 R420 (16.5")*
Front brake: *Brembo, radial 4x34 caliper, two 320mm or 290mm floating discs*
Rear brake: : *Brembo, 4x24 or 2x34 caliper, one 200mm or 218mm vented floating disc*
Weight: *165kg /364lb (with oil and water)*
Fuel capacity: *23.9 litres*

Left - Brembo brakes and discs combine to stop this projectile, whilst Öhlins TTX20 front suspension units take the full force.

Above - The familiar Termignoni exhaust silencer at the rear of the machine.

Right - Öhlins TTX36 rear shock is neatly tucked away between the trestle frame.

The Ducati 999 FO6 represents a further development of the famous twin cylinder 4-stroke L-twin engine, and the perfection of the tubular trestle frame, now synonymous with Ducati. The slender 165kg/364lb engine, coupled with its amazing 194hp, can achieve a staggering straight-line speed in excess of 312kph/194mph.

Harley-Davidson XR-TT 1972 750cc

After decades of dominance in American sport, the native Harley-Davidson factory came under mounting pressure from foreign makers in the seventies. In 1969, the Milwaukee factory had virtually monopolised the multi-discipline US Grand National series. Factory rider Cal Rayborn had won the Daytona 200 and dirt track specialist Mert Lawwill topped the overall championship.

Their 750cc KR V-twins had side-valve cylinder heads, not seen in European sport since the early twenties. Since the thirties the AMA (governing body of US sport) had framed the rules to discourage special works bikes in the interests of privateers. Side-valvers could be of 750cc, while overhead valve or overhead cam engines were restricted to a 500cc maximum.

From 1969, however, an across the board 750cc limit was adopted for dirt racing on flat tracks and a similar de-restriction made for US road racing from 1970.

Harley race chief Dick O'Brien, man behind the phenomenal 150mph KRs, fielded stopgap XR overhead valve 750cc V-twins from 1970. The early XR engine with iron cylinders and heads was based on the aging XL roadster design. It was a disappointment, particularly in road racing, where it lacked both speed and durability. Rayborn's terrific performances in the 1972 UK Transatlantic Match Races on an unofficial iron XR were an exceptional success.

Italian grand prix rider Renzo Pasolini, who was contracted to Harley-Davidson's subsidiary Aermacchi, at speed on a factory XR750 equipped with twin disc front brakes. 'Paso' was fourth overall in the two-leg 1972 Champion Classic run at Ontario raceway near Los Angeles.

A team led by O'Brien, which included Dutch-born engineer Peter Zylstra and gas-flow wizard CR Axtell, undertook a complete redesign of the XR for 1972. The more modern unit had aluminium heads and barrels with larger fin area, shorter connecting rods, pairs of valves disposed at a narrow 68 degrees instead of 90, and compression ratio up from 9.5:1 to 10.5:1.

Not homologated by the AMA in time for the Daytona season-opener, the new XR engine nevertheless took Mark Brelsford to a Grand National title and Cal Rayborn was victorious on the XR-TT road race version in two national rounds, including the first to be held at Laguna Seca, California.

One XR-TT was dispatched to Italy in mid-1972. Since 1960 Harley-Davidson had owned the Aermacchi marque and the Milwaukee factory wanted the Varese factory's experienced GP rider, Renzo Pasolini, to try the V-twin. After Italian race outings, Pasolini and his XR flew to the big US season-ender at Ontario, California. Placing sixth and fourth in the event's two 100-mile legs, the slightly-built but tough Italian took third place overall.

Harley experienced a cruel year in 1973. 'Paso' was killed racing in the 250cc Italian GP and Brelsford was sidelined by injuries sustained in a spectacular fiery crash with another rider at Daytona. At the end of the year, Rayborn was killed riding a Suzuki in New Zealand. On top of these misfortunes, it was clear that the thundering V-twin was being outpaced in Formula 750 racing by fast-improving Japanese two-strokes.

Milwaukee's road racing campaign ended, but the XR engine went on to enjoy an amazingly long career in oval-track dirt racing, where its shape and power characteristics were ideal for the job.

Specifications

Make/Model: *Harley-Davidson XR-TT*

Engine type:
Air-cooled, 45-degree V-twin ohv four-stroke.
Displacement: *749cc*
Fuel system: *2 x 38mm Mikuni VM carburettors*
Ignition: *Fairbanks-Morse magneto*
Lubrication system: *dry sump*
Maximum power: *80ps @ 7,600rpm*
Maximum speed: *155mph/250km/h*

Transmission:
Gearbox: *5-speed*
Primary drive: *chain*
Clutch: *wet, multi-plate*
Final drive: *chain*

Chassis and Running Gear:
Frame type: *tubular double cradle*
Front suspension: *telescopic fork*
Rear suspension: *tubular swingarm with twin shocks*
Front/rear wheels: *wire spoked type 18in*
Front/rear tyres: *Avon 110/80, 130/70*
(Goodyear in period)
Front brake: *240mm double twin-leading-shoe drum*
Rear brake: *single 254mm disc*
Weight: *150kg (330lb)*
Fuel capacity: *24 litres*

Aluminium cylinder heads have generous finning to aid air cooling. Drum brake on this machine is Italian, carburettors are Japanese.

A heat shield on the high-level exhaust pipes protects rider's leg. Large seat fairing provides efficient aerodynamics for high-speed circuits like Daytona Speedway.

Harley-Davidson
XR 1980 750cc

Flat track racing is one of America's most popular forms of motorcycle racing, characterised by breathtaking contests between bunches of riders on evenly matched machines. Events are staged on dirt ovals and on the longer half-mile and one-mile tracks, Harley-Davidson's thundering XR750 has been dominant since the seventies.

The XR's 45-degree V-twin engine has the right qualities for dirt tracking. Its uneven power impulses make for excellent traction and a heavy, narrow crankshaft provides weight distribution beneficial to handling.

The turns are taken in a lurid foot-down power-slide with the steering on opposite lock in speedway style. Typical flat tracker features are high and wide handlebars, small fuel tanks, high-level exhausts and the location of both brake and gear change foot controls on the right. There is no front brake, but a rear brake is compulsory for safety and riders can use its application as part of their sliding technique.

Frames from proprietary makers are used, C&J being one of the most popular brands.

The sole of the left boot, which spends much of its time on the track, is protected by a steel 'hot shoe'. Track surfaces vary from the softer 'cushion' type to a more predictable hard material that enables very close group riding, known as a 'freight train'.

Harley introduced the ohv XR unit in 1970, to replace the side-valve KR twin that had been the main force in flat track since the mid-fifties. However, it was after a redesign for 1972 that the engine started on its long career of success.

Continual development and updating, the most effective being carried out by the factory, saw the XR's power output rise from the 80ps of 1972 to exceed three figures. Chassis improvements were also important and a major flat tracking landmark was reached in 1980, when Hank Scott recorded the first 100mph lap of a one-mile oval at DuQuoin, Illinois - on an XR750, naturally.

Seen here is a 1980 example of the now legendary Harley-Davidson XR750. This machine was purpose-built for dirt-track racing and during its development period resulted in a power output of over 100bhp. This particular machine wears the notorious number 9 of the legendary rider Jay Springsteen.

During the eighties, Harley was challenged by rival V-twin engines from Yamaha and Honda. The latter company deposed the Milwaukee factory four times in the Grand National series between 1985 and 1993 with its purpose-built RS750 V-twin motor.

But in the long run, the evergreen XR prevailed and still dominates the mile ovals in today's Grand National championships.

This example, dating from 1980, was raced by legendary Harley racer Jay Springsteen. Michigan-born 'Springer' shot to fame by winning the US Grand National championship in 1976 when aged 19 and he scooped the title again in the following two years.

Like the Harley engine, Springsteen enjoyed an unusually long track career. He notched up a record 43 National wins, always with Milwaukee hardware, and despite a stress-related stomach complaint, he continued racing at top level until 2003. A great crowd favourite, Springer usually received a standing ovation from the spectators' stand when he came out on the track.

Prior to 1986, the AMA governing body's Grand National series was a multi-discipline championship, with points scored in road racing and TT scrambles events as well as on flat ovals.

Specifications

Make/Model: *Harley-Davidson XR750*

Engine type:
Air-cooled, 45-degree V-twin ohv four-stroke.
Displacement: *749cc*
Fuel system: *: 2 x 38mm Mikuni VM carburettors*
Ignition: *battery and coils with twin-plug heads*
Lubrication system: *dry sump*
Maximum power: *90ps @ 8,000rpm*
Maximum speed: *130mph/250km/h*

Transmission:
Gearbox: *5-speed*
Primary drive: *chain*
Clutch: *wet, multi-plate*
Final drive: *chain*

Chassis and Running Gear:
Frame type: *tubular double cradle*
Front suspension: *telescopic fork*
Rear suspension: *tubular swingarm with twin shocks*
Front/rear wheels: *wire spoked type 19in*
Front/rear tyres: *Carlisle 275 3.75 x 19in*
Front brake: *not fitted*
Rear brake: *254mm disc*
Weight: *n/a*
Fuel capacity: *7.5 litres*

The big-bore twin exhaust pipes (top) exit from the V-Twin engine of the XR750. The twin Mikuni carburettors have large air filters (bottom) to stop dirt entering the engine, a major hazard for any dirt track machine.

Easily identifiable telescopic front forks can be seen here
(top), along with the small sportster style tank and wide bars.
The number nine race plate is part of the housing for the
exhaust, which is neatly tucked behind it to protect the rider.

Honda RC174 1967 297cc

No sooner had Honda got a grip on the smaller capacity GP classes in the mid-sixties than it came under attack from the rapidly improving two-strokes of rival Japanese factories. The four-stroke maker's response to Suzuki and Yamaha was to continue the line of development begun at the start of the decade: multiply cylinders and gain rpm.

In 1964 Honda lost the 250cc crown to Yamaha's 145mph disc-valve twin, demonstrating that its RC164 four was obsolete. Although Honda was preoccupied with a Formula One car racing programme, a response to the speedy two-strokes was produced in time for the late-season Italian GP. The new machine was flown from Japan as carry-on luggage across a row of passenger seats and concealed from view until 250cc practice began at Monza. When team rider Jim Redman wheeled it out, the six exhaust megaphones caused a sensation.

The six-cylinder RC165 was designed by brilliant young Honda engineer Shoichiro Irimajiri. Retaining the in-line transverse format and inclined cylinders of the fours, it was a masterpiece of miniaturisation, with gear-driven overhead camshafts operating 24 little valves like roofing nails. Irimajiri had already ventured into the realms of tiny cylinders and valves by fielding eight-valve twins in the 50cc class.

The six-cylinder unit, featuring a cylinder block integral with the upper crankcase and a wet sump oiling system, was fitted into a conventional tubular open-bottomed frame. When clothed with a fairing the RC165 machine was remarkably slim, with only the six exhaust megaphones to indicate that it wasn't a four, or even a twin.

Mike Hailwood winning the 1967 Lightweight TT on Honda's 250cc six. He rode the complex yet compact machine to two 250cc world championships in 1966 and 1967, also collecting the 1967 350cc title on the enlarged 297cc version. After 1967, Honda took a ten-year break from official GP racing.

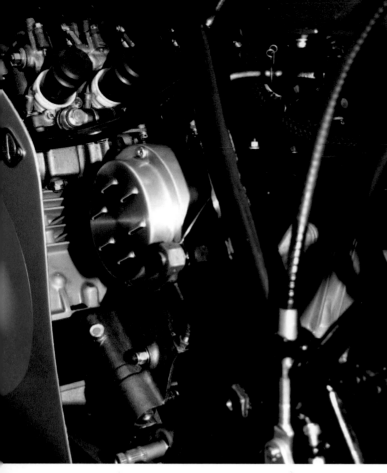

Not a period Six, this is a faithful replica of the 1967 297cc
RC174 built by George Beale in the UK using an 'escaped'
factory bike as a pattern. The noise from the six exhaust
megaphones is fully authentic, too!

Incredibly noisy, the 250cc six could rev to 17,000rpm but early performances were disappointing, marred by misfires and terrible handling. Reliability was improved by fitting a pair of oil cooling radiators in the leading edge of the fairing sides and a seven-speed gearbox replaced the six-speeder. When Mike Hailwood switched from MV Agusta to Honda at the end of 1965 he helped sort the chassis, insisting on British Girling rear shocks.

In 1966 'Mike the Bike' and the six trounced Yamaha's latest V4 two-stroke to win 10 out of 12 GP rounds and regain the 250cc title for Honda. For 1967, a revised RC166 six was joined by a 297cc RC174 version for the 350cc class. Hailwood secured Honda's sixth consecutive 350cc world championship on the enlarged six, with first, and Irish team-mate Ralph Bryans third in the points table behind MV Agusta's Giacomo Agostini. Apart from having its crankshaft stroke lengthened from 31.5mm to 37.5mm and slightly larger Keihin carburettors, the RC174 was essentially similar to the 250cc machine, sharing its light weight and small frontal area.

Since the late nineties, several faithful replicas of the RC174 have been built by UK racing specialist George Beale. He used a machine acquired by a Japanese enthusiast as a pattern and entrusted most of the engine work to a French company. Honda Japan not only gave permission for the replication, but purchased the first machine to be completed.

Oil coolers located in the leading edges of the fairing proved necessary for reliability.

Specifications

Make/Model: *Honda RC174*

Engine type:
Air-cooled in-line four cylinder dohc four-stroke
Displacement: *297cc (41 x 37.5mm)*
Fuel system: *6 x 23mm Keihin carburettors*
Ignition: *Kokusan magneto*
Lubrication system: *dry sump*
Maximum power: *65ps @ 17,000rpm*
Maximum speed: *156mph/252km/h*

Transmission:
Gearbox: *7-speed*
Primary drive: *gears*
Clutch: *multi-plate, dry*
Final drive: *chain*

Chassis and Running Gear:
Frame type: *tubular, engine as stressed member*
Front suspension: *telescopic fork*
Rear suspension: *swingarm with twin shocks*
Front/rear wheels: *wire-spoked 18in*
Front/rear tyres: *Avon 3.00 x 18in/3.25 x 18in*
Front brake: *2 x 200mm twin-leading-shoe drums*
Rear brake: *200mm twin-leading-shoe drum*
Weight: *120kg (265lb)*
Fuel capacity: *22 litres*

Honda RC162 1961 250cc

Nineteen sixty-one was the year when Honda really arrived on the Grand Prix scene. The company, almost unknown outside Japan when it had first raced in Europe two years earlier, clinched world championships in the 125cc and 250cc classes.

Honda's quarter-litre contenders displayed the boldest technology seen in GP racing since the Guzzi V8 of the fifties. With four tiny cylinders and sixteen minuscule valves, they could rev safely to 16,000rpm and emitted an ear-splitting scream from their exhaust megaphones.

They had evolved from Honda's first 250cc four, the RC160, which raced on Japan's unsurfaced Asama track in 1959. It had vertical cylinders with shaft and bevel drive to twin overhead camshafts and an ungainly leading-link front fork.

The RC161 that made its GP debut in 1960 was much revised, with inclined cylinders and camshaft drive by central gears between the inner two cylinders. The front fork was now a conventional telescopic type.

Two talented Australians, Bob Brown and Tom Phillis, were signed to join Honda's Japanese riders in a GP campaign.

The noisy fours showed potential, but erratic performance indicated that more development was needed and Italy's MV Agustas remained aloof in the 250cc championship. However, some pundits' predictions that the fours must be fragile were confounded when three RC161s completed the 189-mile Lightweight TT.

Scottish TT maestro Bob McIntyre on his RC162 four in the 1961 250cc Lightweight race, wearing a battered-looking helmet. He howled round the Mountain Course at 99.58mph to shatter the lap record but an oil leak caused his engine to seize on the last lap. Victory went to Mike Hailwood on a leased RC162, ahead of permanent Honda squad members Tom Phillis and Jim Redman on their fours.

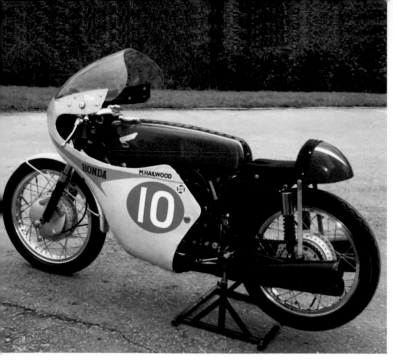

The team returned to Europe for 1961 with further improved RC162 fours. They triumphed at the early-season 250cc West German GP, where Kunimitsu Takahashi won at record speed to become the first Japanese rider to win a world championship race. Rhodesian Jim Redman, who had joined Honda during 1960, was second.

Honda went on to blitz the 250cc Lightweight TT, taking the first five places. The winner was the brilliant young Mike Hailwood whose wealthy father had leased an RC162. He took the flag after Honda team rider Bob McIntyre's machine dropped out when leading. The Scot had shattered the lap record with a circuit at 99.58mph, faster than the standing 350cc record, but his engine seized on the last lap.

The oil level had run low after lubricant had leaked for much of the race and McIntyre had struggled with an oily rear tyre. The RC162 featured dry sump lubrication with an external oil tank in place of an under-engine sump. This enabled the engine to be set lower in the frame to aid handling.

Hailwood had won the 125cc race earlier that day, when Honda twins also took the first five places. He went on to take the 250cc title, while permanent Honda teamster Tom Phillis collected 125cc honours.

MV Agusta knew when they were beaten and the Italian company's 250cc twins were withdrawn by mid-season. It was clear to everyone that the emergent Honda factory not only had bold ideas about engine design, but had the capacity to improve and develop its designs rapidly.

The pioneering transverse in-line fours set a pattern for larger capacity Honda racers and later the typical Japanese four-cylinder roadster.

*Before Honda, no-one had thought that a 16-valve four-
cylinder engine could be so compact.*

Honda NS500 1983

When Freddie Spencer crossed the line to finish second in the 1983 San Marino 500GP, the season's final round, the American became not only the youngest champion in the premier class at the age of 21, he gave Honda their first 500cc title. The previous year he had given the company their first 500cc win since 1967. But Honda's return to winning ways at blue riband level was a long and often tortuous one.

Honda quit GP racing at the end of 1967 because race regulations restricting bikes to four cylinders made their four-stroke machines uncompetitive against increasingly reliable two-strokes. Honda had an almost religious devotion to the four-stroke and indeed their return to 500GPs in 1979 was with an oval-pistoned V4 four-stroke, the NR500. However in competitive terms it was an unmitigated disaster and Honda eventually had to admit defeat and realised they would have to abandon their four-stroke obsession if they were serious about winning the 500cc crown. So the NS500 was born.

Shinichi Miyakoshi was the engineer in charge of the project and he opted for a V3 layout with the two outer cylinders pointing up and the central one pointing downwards, the V angle being 110 degrees and the conrods connected to a single crank. Many questioned his wisdom at the time as the front runners on other manufacturers' bikes were running four-cylinder, twin-crank two-stroke engines and even then were complaining of a lack of power. Also called into question was his use of reed valves instead of the more accurate disc valve induction.

But Miyakoshi had observed that the smaller 350cc bikes were lapping almost as fast as the 500s. His idea was to pursue light weight and ease of use before sheer, brute power. He was vindicated from the very first round of the 1982 season. Spencer was third behind the Yamahas of Kenny Roberts and Barry Sheene in Argentina while team-mate Marco Lucchinelli set the fastest lap at the next round in Austria. Despite being down on power the Hondas were lighter and easier to handle, especially when an aluminium frame was specified from mid-season. Other weight-saving components were carbon fibre wheels with magnesium hubs, reducing unsprung weight to give the suspension an easier time and making for less gyroscopic effect for easier steering.

Freddie Spencer on the NS500 in the Italian Grand Prix in 1982. He finished second in the race to Suzuki's Franco Uncini. Two rounds later he would win in Belgium closing a gap for Honda of 15 years without a Grand Prix victory. The following season he would become the youngest ever GP champion at just 21 years old.

The breakthrough came with Spencer's victory in Belgium. The team's third rider, Takazumi Katayama won again in Sweden. Spencer finished the 1982 series in third place and the scene was set for 1983. A fourth rider joined the team, Ron Haslam. During the close season Honda replaced the constant loss ignition system with a generator-based one and revised the weight distribution to give the riders more front-end confidence.

Honda dominated the first half of the 1983 season, Spencer winning the first three rounds and leading a Honda one-two-three (Spencer, Lucchinelli, Haslam) in the second round at Le Mans. But by mid-season it was the Yamaha of Roberts that was becoming dominant.

That's where good old-fashioned heroics came into play, Spencer riding the wheels off the NS500 to keep it up there, only twice failing to finish in the top three all season.

Either of Roberts or Spencer could have been world champ as they entered the last round in Italy, but even if Roberts won, he needed Spencer to finish third or lower. As it was, Spencer's second behind Roberts gave him the series by just two points, 144 to Roberts 142.

Specifications

Make/Model: *Honda NS500*

Engine type:
Liquid-cooled, V3 two-stroke.
Displacement: *498.7cc (62.6 x 54mm)*
Fuel system: *3 x 36mm cylindrical Mikuni carburettors*
Ignition: *Electronic*
Lubrication system: *two-stroke*
Maximum power: *130ps*
Maximum speed: *180mph*

Transmission:
Gearbox: *6-speed*
Primary drive: *gear*
Clutch: *dry, multi-plate*
Final drive: *chain*

Chassis and Running Gear:
Frame type: *twin loop rectangular aluminium tubing*
Front suspension: *Showa telescopic fork with mechanical anti-dive*
Rear suspension: *swingarm with Showa monoshock*
Front/rear wheels: *16in carbon/magnesium composite*
Front/rear tyres: *Michelin 3.50/4.00*
Front brake: *2 x 300mm steel discs*
Rear brake: *220mm carbon fibre disc*
Weight: *115kg/254lbs*
Fuel capacity: *NA*

Aluminium frame (top) meant less weight and helped to alleviate the triple's power disadvantage compared to the four-cylinder bikes of the competition thanks to a better power to weight ratio. RPM and coolant temperature (left) all a racer in the early 80s really needed to know. Peak power chimed in at 11,000rpm.

NS team leader Shinichi Miyakoshi had been prominent in the development of Honda's motocross bikes and so understood the importance of balance in a competition bike. He was able to make the wheelbase short and keep the frontal area down by using a V3 engine, so although a full 500 the bike rode more like the easier-to-handle 350s. Below, you can clearly see the two rear cylinders and their pipes. Originally square section, the rear expansion chambers were changed to cylindrical. Variable exhaust valves altered their capacity to optimise power delivery.

Honda VFR750R RC30

1989 750cc

Intended as a homologation machine for the World Superbike championship inaugurated in 1988, the Honda V4 was instantly known by its RC30 factory code. It was derived from both the VFR750 roadster and the RVF works endurance racer. The RC30 wasn't immensely powerful but was admirably suited to very fast riding and made a perfect tool for teams and privateers.

American rider Fred Merkel showed the Honda's fitness for Superbike competition by winning the series in 1988 and 1989 on a Team Rumi RC30 with limited factory support. The opposition included full-works Bimota and Ducati hardware.

The V4's flexibility and ease of handling made it an outstanding performer on public roads circuits, especially the Isle of Man TT course. Honda Britain RC30s blitzed the 1988 TT races. They took the first four places in the TT Formula One race, won by Joey Dunlop at record speed on a race-kitted, rather than full-factory, bike. Scottish ace Steve Hislop notched his first TT win in the 750cc Production race on a stock example and Dunlop cleaned up again in the Senior finale.

The factory-prepared RC30 seen here was ridden to a 1989 TT Formula One victory by Hislop, who made history with the first 120mph lap of the 37.73-mile Mountain Course. The second and fourth men home, Brian Morrison and reigning TT F1 champion Carl Fogarty also hit the 'ton-twenty' on RC30s. Dunlop was sidelined by injuries.

Steve Hislop, eventual winner and with head tucked below the screen of his RC30, approaches
the corner at the bottom of Creg ny Baa, during the F1 TT race in 1989.

'Hizzy' went on to win the Villa Real and Ulster TT F1 rounds on this bike, which was taken over by James Whitham to ride on UK circuits in the 1990 season.

RC30s growled to another five more TT wins, including two by new Irish star Phillip McCallen in 1992 and 1993. Fogarty collected another TT F1 title and won the downgraded TT F1 FIM Cup in 1991. Meanwhile many privateers significantly improved their personal best TT lap times, thanks to the RC30's capability. The RC30's final major success was Troy Corser's 1993 Australian Superbike title.

Basically a finely-honed racer in road-legal trim, the RC30 has a VFR750-based 90-degree vee engine with 16 valves. Each pair of camshafts is driven by a train of gears between the cylinders. The single crankshaft carries pairs of big-ends on two common crankpins, disposed at 360 degrees, while the connecting rods are made in light, tough titanium. Twin lightweight radiators tuck snugly into the sleek fairing.

The tidy and compact chassis concentrates weight at the centre of the machine for agile handling and features a robust aluminium twin-spar frame with Honda Pro-Arm rear suspension. Its massive single cast-alloy swinging arm on the left side of the machine was originally designed for rapid wheel changes during endurance races. Quick-release fixings for the front wheel spindle have the same origins.

For 1993, Honda introduced the RC30's successor, the fuel-injected RVF 750R RC45. Although superbly engineered, it failed to make the same impact in racing.

The road-legal RC30 has become a cult machine, sometimes billed as the best motorcycle ever made.

The introduction of the new World Superbike Championship in 1988 along with the stipulated regulations dictating that the machines to be raced should be available to the general public, prompted Honda to develop a new production motorcycle from the existing RVF750 works endurance and Superbike racer. This became the RC30, and although road legal and technically a production motorcycle, it was in reality a racing motorcycle.

The machines were equipped with little in the way of instrumentation (right). Due to the one-sided swingarm, the up-flowing exhaust and rear shock can clearly be seen here (middle right).

The radiator for the twin overhead cam, liquid-cooled, 748cc V-4 engine (bottom), which was housed in an aluminium frame.

Specifications

Make/Model: 750cc Honda VFR750R RC30

Engine type:
Water-cooled, V4 16-valve dohc four-stroke.
Displacement: 748cc (70 x 48.6mm)
Fuel system: 4 x 35mm Keihin carburettors
Ignition: CDI
Lubrication system: wet sump
Maximum power: 112ps @ 11,000rpm (standard trim)
Maximum speed: 158mph/254km/h (standard trim)

Transmission:
Gearbox: 6-speed
Primary drive: gears
Clutch: multi-plate
Final drive: chain

Chassis and Running Gear:
Frame type: aluminium twin-spar
Front suspension: telescopic fork, fully adjustable
Rear suspension: monoshock with one-sided arm, fully adjustable
Front/rear wheels: cast alloy 17in/18in
Front/rear tyres: 120/70x 17in/170/60 x 18in
Front brake: 2 x 300mm discs, four piston calipers
Rear brake: 220mm drum
Weight: 200kg (441lb)
Fuel capacity: 18 litres

Honda RS125 1991 125cc

An ideal machine for the ambitious novice setting out on a road racing career, Honda's RS125 has also been a mainstay of Grand Prix grids since the late eighties, when the FIM made single-cylinder engines compulsory in the 125cc class.

The little Honda has a simple water-cooled two-stroke engine with reed-valve induction. It is housed in a light but rigid aluminium frame, with monoshock rear suspension. Skinny-spoked wheels, drilled brake discs and a miniaturised final drive chain all help keep dry weight below 70kg.

With such a small engine, torque is in short supply, so the rider must develop a technique where the narrow power band can be used to best effect. Maintaining speed in corners is vital, as is not losing momentum by unnecessary shutting of the throttle or over-use of the brakes. Staying tucked in behind the fairing is also advisable, to reduce wind resistance. Slow up for a mere fraction of a second and you can instantly drop several places.

The availability of the RS125 from 1988 as an over-the-counter racer was behind a general revival of 125cc racing. It included the restoration of an Ultra Lightweight race at the Isle of Man TT in 1989, after it had been absent from the programme for 15 years.

This 1991 example was raced in the TT by the most successful Isle of Man racer in history, Joey Dunlop. His sponsor in the smallest class was Andy McMenemy, a motor trader from County Antrim.

The little Honda RS125 is an ideal starter machine for any novice wanting to get into motorcycle racing. Seen here in 1991 is the late great Joey Dunlop, who became the most successful Isle of Man racer in history.

No doubting who raced this little RS125 - Joey was a legend in his own lifetime and this machine helped him to gain that status. Sadly he was also killed on a Honda RS125 in 2000 while racing in the Kalevi Suursoit event at the 3.7 mile (4.3km) woodland road race circuit in Tallinn, Estonia. This machine is now lovingly looked after and kept in a private collection in Ireland.

Dunlop was seriously injured in a crash at Brands Hatch in 1989 and that, combined with his approaching the age of 40, made it look as though his amazing career was in decline. But after missing one year, he returned to the TT in 1990 and it was in the 125cc Ultra Lightweight race that he showed he hadn't lost his touch. He duelled for second place with fellow Honda rider Ian Newton, before breaking down on the last of the three laps. The race winner was Joey's younger brother Robert and many subsequent 125cc TTs would be battles between the two Dunlops.

The two lined up to face a damp Mountain Course in the 1991 Ultra Lightweight, with Joey on this machine. He took the lead from Robert and had pulled out 25 seconds when the fuel tank's breather tube - which allows air in as the tank empties - came adrift. With vision hampered by petrol streaming over the fairing screen and his helmet visor, Joey had to slow and Robert beat him to the chequered flag by 40 seconds.

Joey turned the tables by winning the 1992 125cc TT. He went on to win again in 1993, 1994, 1996 and 2000, demonstrating exceptional finesse in 125cc racing. His victories and Robert's four in the class were all on Honda RS125Rs, which had a virtual monopoly in the Ultra Lightweight TT until it was discontinued after 2002.

By then the amazing featherweight was producing well in excess of 40ps and the RS125R is still going strong on the track, from club level up to Moto GP.

The mouth of a carburettor can be seen tucked away inside the beautifully welded frame (top); instrumentation is minimal (bottom).

Specifications

Make/Model: *125cc Honda RS125R*

Engine type:
Water-cooled, single cylinder piston-port two-stroke.
Displacement: *124cc (54 x 54.5mm)*
Fuel system: *38mm Keihin carburettor*
Ignition: *CDI magneto*
Lubrication system: *petroil*
Maximum power: *39ps @ 12,000rpm*
Maximum speed: *130mph/209km/h (dependent on gearing)*

Transmission:
Gearbox: *6-speed*
Primary drive: *gears*
Clutch: *wet, multi-plate*
Final drive: *chain*

Chassis and Running Gear:
Frame type: *tubular, double cradle*
Front suspension: *telescopic fork*
Rear suspension: *monoshock*
Front/rear wheels: *cast alloy 17in*
Front/rear tyres: *Michelin 9x58x17/12x59x17in*
Front brake: *296mm disc*
Rear brake: *186mm disc*
Weight: *68kg (150lb)*
Fuel capacity: *12 litres*

Repsol Honda RC211V
2006

Headlines in MCN (Motor Cycle News) at the beginning of the 2006 MotoGP season, were right on the button when they announced that reigning MotoGP World Champion Valentino Rossi was struggling with vibration problems on his all-new 2006 Yamaha M1. The problem was to plague Rossi throughout most of the season, even though it was finally resolved.

Honda's Nicky Hayden on the other hand was getting to grips with the RC211V, along with his very fast team-mate Dani Pedrosa. In fact it was Pedrosa who would take second place ahead of Hayden at the opening race on the Jerez circuit in Spain. But as the season progressed, Hayden became more consistent, and as Rossi struggled to tame the Yamaha, he would steadily accumulate enough championship points to pull away from his biggest rival. As Rossi returned to

his winning ways, the outcome of the championship went to the wire and was decided at the seventeenth and final round in Valencia. So unlike him, Rossi fell from his bike, and although the plucky Italian re-mounted and raced for his life, he was unable to capture the points needed to overtake Hayden.

The RC211V (RC - Honda's traditional racing prefix , 211 - first works bike of the twenty-first century, and 'V' denoting the engine configuration) had been developed during 2001 to replace the highly successful NSR500. This was due to regulation changes which allowed two-stroke engines to be limited to 500cc with four-cylinders, whilst on the other hand four-stroke engines would be allowed to increase their capacity up to 990cc, with a span of three to six cylinders. The class name was also changed to MotoGP, and was limited to race prototypes only.

One of the closest MotoGP title fights ended in victory for Nicky Hayden (Repsol Honda RC211V) at Valencia at the end of the 2006 season. Third place was enough for the 'Kentucky Kid' to end the reign of Valentino Rossi (Yamaha) who had a spill on lap five.

Left - Carbon is the common denominator for the front brakes on the 211V. The twin Brembo discs seen here, and the brake pads hidden in the four pot calipers are all made of this material.
Bottom - Instrumentation is simple and easy to read. Although the rider will consult it, he is generally totally aware of what is happening without having to check constantly.
Right - The RC211V, World Championship MotoGp machine. This is the bike that Nicky Hayden rode to win his world title for the 2006 season.

The RC211V made its debut in 2002 and was a unique machine in the respect that it used a V5 engine. The four-stroke unit, with its three cylinders to the front and two to the rear, also had an innovative exhaust pipe system to cope with the strange configuration. Considerable attention was also paid to the fairing, which is small and said to be un-aerodynamic. The reason for this was that Honda had discovered that the advantage gained by a big fairing in a straight line came at the expense of cornering stability. The smaller fairing would also give better access to mechanicals during the race.

With its claimed 240-plus hp, and a speed in excess of 213mph (340km/h), Valentino Rossi had dominated the 2002 MotoGP season and romped home with the championship. He won it once again on the RC211V in 2003, before moving to Yamaha and being crowned on further occasions.

So for 2006, the RC211V that had been developed in the capable hands of Rossi, was taken over by Nicky Hayden, who took on the mantle of team leader. He was no stranger to the machine, having ridden it in previous seasons. The big question on everybody's mind was, could the 'Kentucky Kid' come up with the goods, and history now shows that in 2006 he did. For 2007 the regulations changed again.

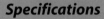

Top - Just the single brake disc is needed on the rear, but the two pot caliper is still required to help stop this projectile.
Bottom - The RC211V has an ingenious rear suspension design, where the rear damper is located within the swingarm, so now much of the space once taken up by the suspension, houses a lower and more centrally positioned fuel tank.

Specifications

Make/Model: *Repsol Honda RC211V 2006*

Engine type:
Liquid-cooled, four-stroke, dohc 4 valve, V5.
Displacement: *990 cc*
Fuel system: *Fuel injection*
Lubrication system: *Semi-dry-sump*
Maximum power: *Over 240hp*
Maximum speed: *180mph (288kp/h)*

Transmission:
Gearbox: *6 speed*
Primary drive: *gear*
Clutch: *Multi plate, wet*
Final drive: *Chain*

Chassis and Running Gear:
Frame type: *twin tube*
Front suspension: *telescopic*
Rear suspension: *New Unit Pro-link*
Front/rear wheels: *16.5 in*
Front/rear tyres: *17in/16.5in*
Front brake: *Carbon discs with four-pot Nissin calipers*
Rear brake: *Single Brembo Steel disc, 2 pot caliper, 230mm disc with AP Lockheed caliper*
Weight: *148 kg*
Fuel capacity: *22 litres*

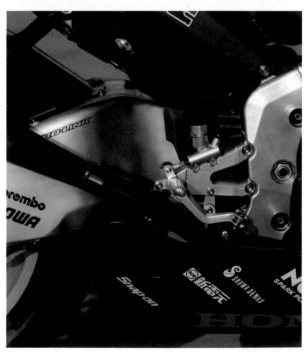

Kawasaki H1-R 1970

Kawasaki conceived the H1-R two-stroke triple as a promotional tool for the crucial American market, hoping to translate race success to showroom sales, but it would be a British rider that would give them their first 500GP win.

The hyper-fast H1 road bike had been launched in the States in late 1968, but poor performances from race-prepped roadsters in the crucial production racing arenas of Daytona, the Isle of Man and the Thruxton 500-miles forced Kawasaki's hand to develop something more competitive. And so the H1-R was developed and went on sale as a short run of 40 bikes in December 1969, just in time for works and factory-supported teams to campaign them in the 1970 season.

Typically for a Japanese bike of the era, the engine was rather more capable than the chassis. With 75bhp at 9,000rpm, the H1-R was certainly a lusty performer, but with a prodigious thirst of around 16mpg and a fuel tank that could carry just five gallons, additional tank capacity had to be provided for most races. Add this to an engine mounted high in the frame to compensate for its width for ground clearance, and the result was a top-heavy race bike that handled badly on twistier circuits.

A regular Kawasaki rider, this is Mick Grant seen at the Senior TT on his H-1R during 1975.
Grant went onto win the event.

That didn't stop Kiwi privateer Ginger Molloy from making his mark on the H1-R. In the second race of the 1970 season at Le Mans he finished second to MV Agusta's Giacomo Agostini and three other second places that year helped him to second place in the 500GP championship. At Daytona, Molloy finished seventh in the 200-mile race, timed on the banking at a blistering 159.83mph, while American privateer Rusty Bradley was the winner of the 100-mile Amateur race. On the Isle of Man, Bill Smith came third in the Senior TT with the assistance of an eight-gallon fuel tank.

Brit Dave Simmonds, the man who had given Kawasaki their first GP title with the 125cc crown in 1969, struggled with the H1-R throughout its debut season but for 1971 he mounted his engine in a frame built by Renolds Tubing legend Ken Sprayson. This was lower, lighter and more rigid than the Kawasaki-supplied item. Simmonds also replaced the standard five-speed box with a six-speed unit.

The modified H1-R showed promise at the season's fourth round, the Dutch TT at Assen, where Simmonds was third behind Agostini and Rob Bron (Suzuki). Second place in Finland and third at Monza boosted his points tally. But it was at the last round in Spain, at Jarama, where Simmonds' H1-R finally came good, winning the race and netting Kawasaki's first 500GP victory. Admittedly the field lacked many of the top stars, who in those days didn't have to ride all of the GP rounds as championship standings were decided on their best results in half of the rounds plus one (seven in 1971). But it was a significant win nonetheless, underscoring the real potential of Kawasaki in racing.

Despite the many shortcomings of the standard H1-R, it set the template for a very successful decade in competition for Kawasaki. The first of a line of Green Meanies had arrived.

In 1970, the H1R was available worldwide as a limited production road racing machine. Kawasaki had had great worldwide racing success with the H1R, and during the 1970 Daytona road race, an H1R piloted by Ginger Molloy was clocked on the banking at 159.83mph - unheard of at the time.

The in-line, three-cylinder, two-stroke engine, neatly tucked under the fuel tank of the H-1R.

The fuel tank could be removed easily and was made of lightweight materials (top). Simple instrumentation consists of tachometer and water temperature gauges (bottom).

Specifications

Make/Model: *Kawasaki H1-R*

Engine type:
Air-cooled, three cylinder two-stroke.
Displacement: *499cc (60 x 58.8mm)*
Fuel system: *3 x VM35SC Mikuni*
Lubrication system: *injected two-stroke plus premix*
Maximum power: *75bhp @ 9,000rpm*
Maximum speed: *160mph/257.5km/h*

Transmission:
Gearbox: *5-speed*
Primary drive: *gear*
Clutch: *dry, multi-plate*
Final drive: *chain*

Chassis and Running Gear:
Frame type: *tubular double cradle*
Front suspension: *telescopic fork*
Rear suspension: *swingarm with twin shocks*
Front/rear wheels: *spoked 18in*
Front/rear tyres: *Yokohama*
Front brake: *250mm drum*
Rear brake: *250mm drum*
Weight: *136kg (dry)*
Fuel capacity: *5 gallons (22.73 litres)*

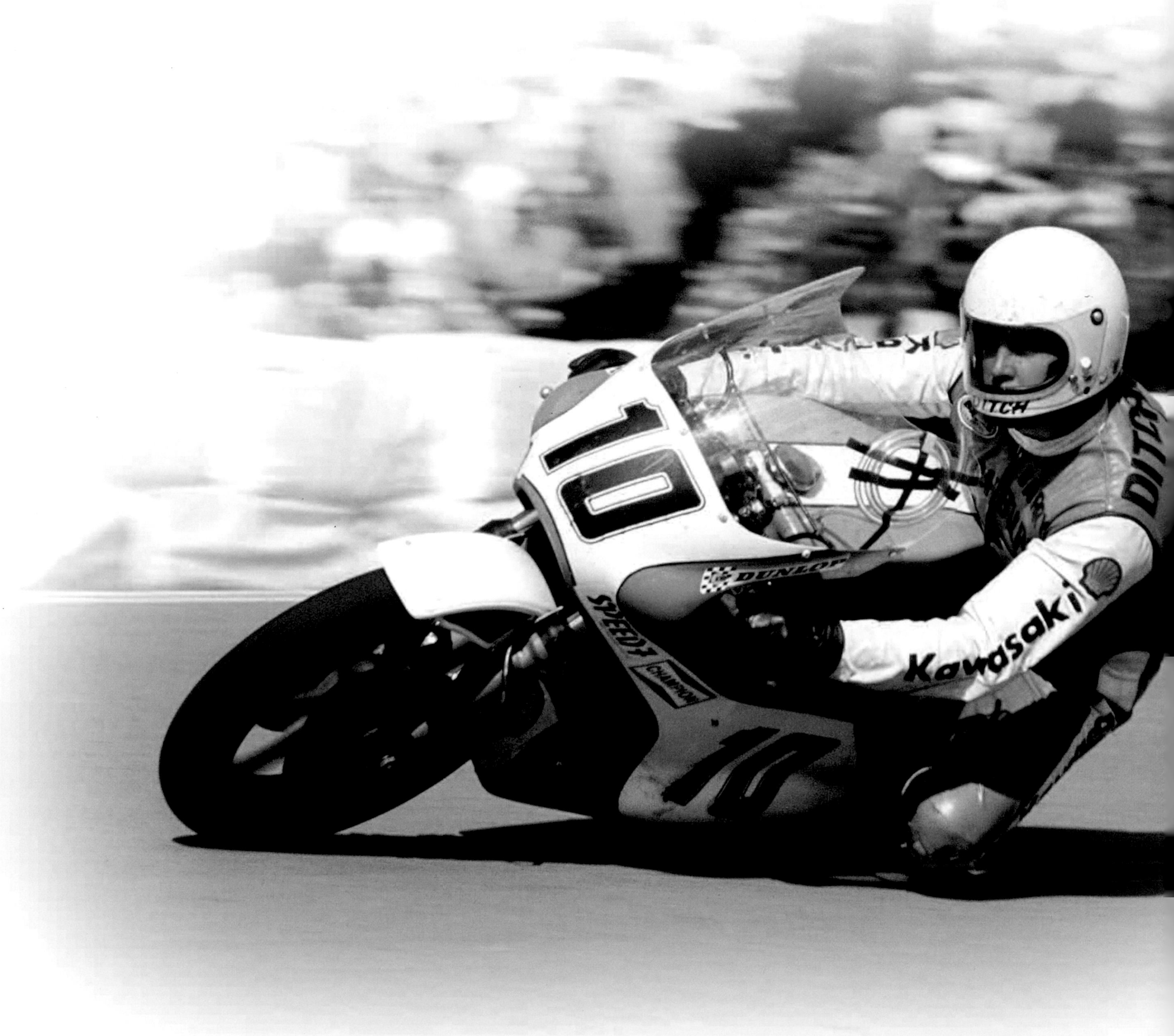
10
DUNLOP
Kawasaki
CHAMPION

Kawasaki KR750
1975 750cc

Kawasaki had built a 750cc racer prior to the KR750 but that bike, the H2-R, was a production racer built to promote the hyper-fast 750cc H2 road-going two-stroke triple introduced in 1972.

It was only when the FIM relaxed the homologation requirements for its 750 Championship at the end of 1974 that Kawasaki felt it could justify the development of a full-house, dedicated 750cc race bike. Where previously the FIM had dictated that 200 machines had to be produced for homologation purposes, they reduced that figure to 25.

There was to be no easy debut for the KR750. Five bikes were entered in the 1975 Daytona 200, but gearbox and crankshaft failures saw them all retire, including the UK Team Boyer Kawasakis of Mick Grant and Barry Ditchburn. Disappointment followed again at the second round of the FIM 750 Championship at Imola, with just Grant finishing, managing fifth in the first race but missing the second one as his mechanics had stripped the motor to check a piston.

Undeterred by the early failures, Team Boyer set about developing the KR, replacing the aluminium brakes with stainless steel, fitting Girling shocks and changing the carbs and expansion chambers and modifying the porting. They soon reaped the rewards in the UK Motorcycle News Superbike series, Grant winning the first two rounds and ultimately becoming series champion with Ditchburn second. On the world stage, Grant's bike seized in Belgium and Ditchburn ran out of fuel while leading. Canadian Yvon DuHamel's KR seized at Magny Cours but he took the KR's first victory in the FIM series with a double in Assen.

Barry Ditchburn aboard a KR750 in the Dutch FIM 750 round at Assen in 1975. He set the equal fastest lap in the race but retired with mechanical difficulties. Fellow KR750 rider Miguel DuHamel won the race giving the KR its maiden victory in the series.

The KR750 may have been made in Japan but it was down to the British Boyer Kawasaki team to do much of the development work on the bike. One of the many things they changed and refined were the carbs (left). Other things taken care of by chief mechanic Nigel Everett included the cylinders which were supplied rough and unported.

On the Isle of Man Grant set a new lap record of 109.82mph, beating the near-decade-old mark of Mike Hailwood. That was in the Open Classic TT but Grant failed to finish when forced to retire because of final drive problems. However Kawasaki had much encouraging cause for celebration at the 1975 TT when Granty took the 500cc H1-RW to victory in the Senior, then still classified as a GP, giving the firm their first blue-riband class win since that of Dave Simmonds in Jarama four years before, in 1971.

Boyer Kawasaki didn't make Daytona for 1976, so it was left to the US team augmented by Australian Team Kawasaki rider Gregg Hansford to fly the flag. Less weight (143kg) and bigger 38mm carbs plus other engine mods should have comfortably sealed the deal, but Kawasaki's success came from tyre problems on the competing Yamaha TZ750s and evergreen American hard man Gary Nixon came second, providing Kawasaki with the KR's best ever result.

In the hands of Nixon, FIM 750 Championship victory beckoned that year, but a controversial loss of points after he used a borrowed engine in Venezuela denied Nixon the title.

Boyer Kawasaki's 1976 wasn't brilliant, but Grant and Ditchburn took the one-two at Brands in the British Superbike Championship, repeating the feat at Oulton Park.

For 1977 the 602L model was down to a dry weight of 136kg and Gregg Hansford managed fourth at Daytona while Grant took second at England's Oulton Park. Grant won the Superbike race at the North-West 200 and set an outright lap record of 112.776mph on his way to the win at the Classic TT.

For its final two seasons the KR was largely outclassed although it could still occasionally worry the competition, and 1979 was its last season.

Make/Model: *Kawasaki KR750*

Engine type:
Liquid-cooled, three cylinder two-stroke.
Displacement: *740cc (68 x 68mm)*
Fuel system: *3 x 35mm Mikuni*
(38mm for 1976)
Lubrication system: *forced two-stroke*
injection
Maximum power: *120bhp @ 9,500rpm*
Maximum speed: *180mph/288kph*

Transmission:
Gearbox: *6-speed*
Primary drive: *gear*
Clutch: *dry, multi-plate*
Final drive: *chain*

Chassis and Running Gear:
Frame type: *tubular double cradle*
Front suspension: *telescopic fork*
Rear suspension: *swingarm with*
twin shocks
Front/rear wheels: *Morris magnesium*
Front/rear tyres: *N/A*
Front brake: *2 x 296mm discs*
Rear brake: *232mm disc*
Weight: *147kg (410lb)*
Fuel capacity: *26 litres*

Just poking into shot on the left of the picture is the steering damper, there to minimise the very worst of the head-shake wobbles. Essential on real roads circuits such as the Isle of Man and the North-West 200.

Kawasaki KR250
1980 250cc

Kawasaki came to the Grand Prix scene later than the other major Japanese factories. British rider Dave Simmonds' one-man campaign gained the company a 125cc world championship in 1969 and New Zealander privateer Ginger Molloy was second in the 500cc series in 1970, both on two-strokes.

In the early seventies, Kawasaki were prominent in the Formula 750 class with three-cylinder two-strokes. Activities were based mainly in America, which is where the KR250 GP-type twin first appeared, at Daytona in 1975.

Clearly a challenger to Yamaha's dominant TZ250, the newcomer differed from it radically. A narrow 'tandem twin', its two water-cooled cylinders were placed one behind the other, with contra-rotating crankshafts geared together. They were slightly offset, allowing the disc valves on the left of the magnesium crankcase to overlap. The exhausts, sited front and rear, made a distinctive low-pitched sound when the tandem twin pulled out of slow corners.

Disc valve induction helped give a useful spread of power. The ignition unit was mounted on the right side of the forward crankshaft while a gear on the rear shaft drove the cooling system's impeller as well as transmitting drive to the gearbox via a multi-plate clutch. Machines prepared for Daytona had seven-speed gearboxes, not permissible under FIM GP rules.

Not an instant success, the KR250 only came good when the crankshafts were arranged so that the pistons rose and fell in unison. That cured severe vibration experienced with the original one-up, one-down timing. The improved engine, with a six-speed gearbox, was fielded in 1977 when Uni-Trak monoshock rear suspension was also introduced.

Kork Ballington races his UK-based KR250 tandem twin in the 1978 Austrian GP. He won the 250cc world championship for Kawasaki in 1978 and 1979, and took the 350cc title on the KR350 derivative in 1978.

Eddie Lawson's 1980 Daytona 250GP race winner. Carburettors feed into crankcase directly, via disc valves to time induction periods.

The UK-based Boyer Kawasaki team clinched the KR250's first world championship wins when Mick Grant won the Dutch and Swedish 250cc rounds. Team Kawasaki Australia's Gregg Hansford won races in the US and New Zealand as well as his native country.

South African rider Kork Ballington, racing with the UK team, narrowly won the 250cc world championship from Hansford in 1978. He also collected the 350cc title on a successfully enlarged version of the KR250. Ballington repeated the double in 1979 and in the following three years Germany's Toni Mang rode Sepp Schlogl-prepared machines to two titles in each class.

Other KR250 riders included Briton Barry Ditchburn, Canadian Yvon DuHamel and American Eddie Lawson, who rode this example. The Californian, who shot to fame in the States riding Kawasaki's unwieldy four-stroke fours to two US Superbike street machine championships, gained excellent results on KR250s fettled by ace tuner Steve Johnson. The quirky tandem engine only performed well if skilfully set up.

Lawson was America's 250 Grand Prix class champion in 1980. He won the Daytona opener on a Yamaha, then switched to the KR250 to top the last three rounds. In the following year he won at Daytona, Elkhart Lake, Loudon and Laguna Seca on the green machine to take a second 250cc title.

At the end of 1982 Kawasaki terminated its GP activities. 'Steady Eddie' Lawson joined Yamaha's GP team for 1983 and gained four 500cc world championships.

Make/Model: *250cc Kawasaki KR250*

Engine type:

Water-cooled, in-line twin disc valve four-stroke.

Displacement: *247cc (54 x 54mm)*
Fuel system: *2 x 34mm Mikuni carburettors*
Ignition: *Kokusan CDI magneto*
Lubrication system: *petroil mix*
Maximum power: *55ps @ 12,000rpm*
Maximum speed: *150mph/241km/h (dependent on gearing)*

Transmission:

Gearbox: *6-speed*
Primary drive: *gears*
Clutch: *dry, multi-plate*
Final drive: *chain*

Chassis and Running Gear:

Frame type: *tubular, double cradle*
Front suspension: *telescopic fork*
Rear suspension: *box-section swingarm with twin shocks*
Front/rear wheels: *Morris cast alloy 18in*
Front/rear tyres: *3.25 x 17in/3.50 x 17in*
Front brake: *310mm discs*
Rear brake: *210mm disc*
Weight: *104kg (230lb)*
Fuel capacity: *23litres*

Plumbing for the cooling system's water impeller, driven off rear crankshaft.

Laverda V6 1978 1000cc

It may have only raced once, when it failed to finish, but Laverda's V6 has achieved legendary status thanks to its sheer technical exuberance. The Italian factory moved from making lightweights to large-capacity motorcycles in the sixties and its high performance roadgoing 750cc twins and 1000cc triples of the seventies were highly rated.

Endurance races, lasting from eight to 24 hours were rapidly growing in popularity in the seventies throughout Continental Europe and Laverda entered twins with a degree of success. Rules insisting on roadster-based machinery were relaxed, allowing 'prototypes' to compete. Honda and Kawasaki teams were fielding pure-bred racers and Laverda rose to the challenge. In 1976 work began on a no-holds-barred endurance contender.

Company boss Massimo Laverda and his chief designer Luciano Zen led the project, in consultation with ex-Maserati engineer Giulio Alfieri. Their car-like water-cooled power unit has two sets of three cylinders disposed at 90-degrees on a common crankshaft set longitudinally. Four valves in each cylinder are operated by overhead camshafts driven by chains from a countershaft, which is itself chain-driven off the crankshaft. Six special carburettors with vertical chokes are within the vee, while the exhaust pipes exit from below, snaking into a single outlet. Oil for the twin-pump dry sump lubrication system is carried in an under-seat tank on the left of the machine, with a battery on the right. Charged by a generator, it powers the electronic ignition and lighting, which includes number plate illumination required for 24-hour racing.

Massimo Laverda and the infamous Laverda V6, seen here at the factory, in northern Italy, discussing road test details with one of his technicians.

A gear drive transmits power to the clutch, which rotates in the opposite direction to the crankshaft. This arrangement, along with a balancer device on the generator shaft, helps counteract torque reactions generated by the longitudinal layout. The five-speed gearbox is on the right of the unit, where a shaft and bevel gear take drive to the rear wheel.

The power unit is a stressed chassis member, connected to the steering head by triangulated tubes. A long, braced swingarm pivots in the crankcase casting, while the upper ends of the twin Marzocchi gas shocks anchor to a subframe supporting the seat. The front fork is also Marzocchi, while the brake calipers are by Brembo.

Although a heavy machine - the power unit alone weighs around 175kg - the Laverda is compactly built and even with minimal development its output was close to 140bhp with a 12,500rpm upper limit.

Displayed at the 1977 Milan Show, the V6 raced in France's annual Bol d'Or 24-hour race at Circuit Paul Ricard in September 1978. The riders were Carlo Perugini and Nico Cereghini. Clocked on the circuit's Mistral straight at over 175mph, the sweet-sounding six circulated for a little over eight hours until the final drive shaft, known by the team to be a weak point, failed.

Hugely expensive, the mighty V6 was said to be a development tool for future Laverda superbikes but it lay fallow until a scheme to build 50 replicas was aired in 1991. But after the company changed hands two years later, hopes of a roadgoing version faded.

Specifications

Make/Model: *1000cc Laverda V6*

Engine type:
Water-cooled, V6 dohc 24-valve four-stroke.
Displacement: *996cc (65 x 50mm)*
Fuel system: *6 x 32mm Dell' Orto vertical choke carburettors*
Ignition: *Marelli electronic*
Lubrication system: *dry sump*
Maximum power: *139ps @ 10,500rpm*
Maximum speed: *175mph/282km/h (estimated)*

Transmission:
Gearbox: *5-speed*
Primary drive: *gears*
Clutch: *dry, single plate*
Final drive: *shaft*

Chassis and Running Gear:
Frame type: *tubular with engine as stressed member*
Front suspension: *telescopic fork*
Rear suspension: *swingarm with twin shocks*
Front/rear wheels: *cast alloy 18in*
Front/rear tyres: *Dunlop Slicks*
Front brake: *2 x 280mm discs with Brembo calipers*
Rear brake: *230mm disc with Brembo caliper*
Weight: *230kg (507lb)*
Fuel capacity: *n/a*

Rear suspension made up of swingarm and twin shocks (left).

The incredibly low slung V6 engine with the six Dell'Orto carburettors and their trumpets look pretty impressive.

Twin large headlamps were a must for endurance racing, which is what this machine was destined for.

The Laverda V6 racer only raced at the Bol D'Or, and although it was the fastest bike in a straight line by several mph, it never finished the race.

Moto Guzzi V8 1957 500cc

Rivalry between proud Italian marques was responsible for a spate of technical creativity in the 1950s. The most remarkable outcome was Moto Guzzi's extraordinary 180mph V8. Guzzi, veterans of Grand Prix racing since the 1920s, were strong in the 250cc and 350cc classes of the FIM world championship inaugurated in 1949. But the company struggled to match Gilera and MV Agusta's transverse fours in the premier 500cc class.

A bought-in longitudinal four-cylinder design tried in 1954-1955 brought mediocre results, so Guzzi's brilliant engineer Giulio Carcano set about designing a world-beater for his free-spending bosses. More cylinders with smaller, lighter pistons meant more rpm and more power impulses for every mile covered, so he reasoned that a six must outpace a four. After further consideration, he decided on a more complex but narrower V8.

Seeking lightness and a small frontal area, Carcano made his liquid-cooled power unit incredibly compact. The cylinder banks were set at a 90-degree angle with eight tiny carburettors between them. Two camshafts on each bank were driven by a train of gears on the right of the unit, while the geared primary drive was on the left.

A one-piece crankshaft with split bearings was tried at first, but during development it was replaced by a more durable built-up type with patent Hirth couplings.

A six-speed gearbox was originally specified but the engine proved to be surprisingly flexible, so four- and five-speed boxes were used. The power unit fitted into a conventional tubular frame, the swingarm pivot being housed in the rear of the massive magnesium crankcase casting.

Dickie Dale rests after finishing fourth in the 300-mile (483km) Senior TT of 1957.
His V8's 'dolphin' fairing is spattered with flies.

MOTO GUZZI V8

The V8 made its GP debut during 1956. Guzzi's English rider Bill Lomas was lying third in the Belgian GP when the ignition failed and in Germany he battled for the lead with Gilera's reigning 500cc world champion Geoff Duke, both riders breaking the lap record. When the Gilera retired Lomas led – until a radiator hose loosened.

After a winter of further work Guzzi pulled off a publicity coup when Lomas hit 178mph (285km/h) in a timed run on a closed public road near Rome. He was sidelined by injuries that year, but other riders had promising early season results in Italy. Giuseppe Colnago won a national race and British Guzzi teamster Dickie Dale took victory at Imola.

Dale was plagued by misfires at the Isle of Man Senior TT, but managed fourth. On Belgium's fast Spa circuit, Australian Guzzi rider Keith Campbell blew off the Gilera and MV teams, pushing the lap record beyond 118mph (190km/h). Then a severed electrical lead silenced the growling V8.

Just when development was bearing fruit and a 350cc version was in prospect, Guzzi withdrew from GP racing. The leading Italian marques had made a pact at the end of 1957 to halt heavy.

 The V8's handling was always in question and the tyres of the day were inadequate for its power. But Lomas always maintained that another season's racing would have seen the Guzzi become invincible.

Specifications

Make/Model: *Moto Guzzi V8*

Engine type:
Liquid-cooled 90-degree V8 dohc four-stroke.
Displacement: *499cc (44 x 41mm)*
Fuel system: *8 x 21mm Dell' Orto carburettors*
Ignition: *battery and coils with cb points*
Lubrication system: *dry sump*
Maximum power: *80ps at 13,000rpm*
Maximum speed: *180mph/290km/h*

Transmission:
Gearbox: *5-speed*
Primary drive: *gears*
Clutch: *multi-plate, dry*
Final drive: *chain*

Chassis and Running Gear:
Frame type: *tubular, spine and double cradle*
Front suspension: *leading-link fork*
Rear suspension: *swingarm with twin shocks*
Front/rear wheels: *wire spoked 19in (rear also 20in)*
Front/rear tyres: *3.00 x 19in/3.25 x 19in (also 20in)*
Front brake: *2 x 220mm drums*
Rear brake: *210mm drum*
Weight: *297lb (135kg)*
Fuel capacity: *25 litres*

Left side of the compact engine, showing ignition points covers on the camshafts, four ignition coils are at left and primary drive casing with dry clutch. Front fork is a leading-link type with detachable shock units.

Australian Guzzi team rider Keith Campbell on the V8. The fairing, with air intakes for the cooling system's radiator, is of the 'full bin' type banned in FIM events from 1958. By then Moto Guzzi had withdrawn from the expensive pursuit of world championships

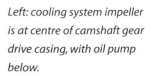

Left: cooling system impeller is at centre of camshaft gear drive casing, with oil pump below.

MV Agusta 1972 750cc

After two decades of supremacy in Grand Prix racing, the standing of the mighty MV Agusta team looked precarious in 1971. Its driving force, the immensely proud Count Domenico Agusta, died in February of that year. He had funded racers that bore no relation to Meccanica Verghera Agusta's modest output of roadsters and the family firm's main business was not motorcycles, but helicopters. The marque's track presence was purely about prestige.

When Domenico's brother Corrado took charge the prospects for racing looked bleak. MV's production motorcycles were unprofitable, the aviation engineers saw the GP team as a drain on resources, and Italian industry in general was going through a period of disputes and stoppages.

Despite all this, Corrado not only gave the go-ahead for the 1972 GP season: he agreed a project that Domenico might not have approved of.

Formula 750, a class for racers based on production roadsters, was taking off on both sides of the Atlantic. In April 1972, Italy staged its answer to America's Daytona epic, a 200-mile race held on the fast Imola circuit.

MV fielded a machine homologated by the company's exclusive four-cylinder 750S Sport. Unveiled at the 1969 Milan Show, the Sport evolved out of a 600cc shaft-drive tourer unsuitable for high-speed work. That was intentional - Count Domenico did not want privateers to race his fours and devalue the Agusta mystique.

Giacomo Agostini during his 1972 Imola ride on the big roadster-based four, when he set joint fastest lap before retiring with machine trouble. The 1972 original has a Ceriani double twin-leading-shoe drum front brake and final drive by shaft.

A high-performance version of the 750S power unit was developed in MV's race shop, run by Arturo Magni. Tuned to breathe through racing carburettors and exhaust via an open megaphone system like that on the GP fours, its crankcase and gearbox cover were lightweight magnesium castings. Weight was also shed by casting the shaft drive's rear bevel box in similar material.

The rider was MV's ten-times world champion Giacomo Agostini. Alberto Pagani practiced on a second bike but did not race.

When the flag dropped Ago shot into the lead and held it for several laps before being hauled in and passed by the Ducati V-twins of Paul Smart and Bruno Spaggiari. He diced for a time with Percy Tait's factory Triumph, but then the MV slowed and stopped. Smart won the race, but Agostini shared the fastest lap with Spaggiari, who finished second.

Although the MV team reported an engine component failure it was widely believed that the problem lay with the shaft drive. Even when functioning properly it added undesirable weight and the torque reactions it set up created serious handling problems that made Agostini's fast lap all the more creditable.

After Imola, MV's race shop had to focus on the Grand Prix campaign, especially in the 350cc class where its dominance was being challenged by Yamaha. Magni devised a chain drive conversion and built a batch of machines so fitted, but MV Agusta did not figure in Formula 750 racing again. It was not until the marque was revived in 1997 that the company's standard over-500cc fours had chain final drive.

Specifications

Make/Model: *1972 750cc MV Agusta*

Engine type:
Air-cooled, in-line, four-cylinder dohc four-stroke.
Displacement: *743cc (65 x 56mm)*
Fuel system: *4 x 27mm Dell' Orto SS carburettors*
Ignition: *Bosch coil and distributor*
Lubrication system: *wet sump*
Maximum power: *85ps @ 9,000rpm (estimated)*
Maximum speed: *158mph/255km/h (estimated)*

Transmission:
Gearbox: *5-speed*
Primary drive: *chain*
Clutch: *dry, single plate*
Final drive: *chain (originally shaft)*

Chassis and Running Gear:
Frame type: *tubular double cradle*
Front suspension: *telescopic fork*
Rear suspension: *swingarm with twin shocks*
Front/rear wheels: *spoked 19in*
Front/rear tyres: *Dunlop KR76 3 x 19in/KR73 3.50 x 19in*
Front brake: *2 x 280mm discs (originally double twin-leading-shoe drum)*
Rear brake: *210mm single-leading-shoe drum*
Weight: *200kg (440lb)*
Fuel capacity: *22 litres*

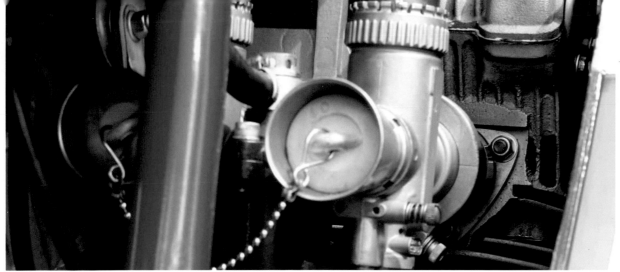

Carburation is by four 27mm Dell' Orto SS carburettors with remote float chambers. Plugs are used to keep foreign bodies out of the intakes when the machine is not running.

This surviving machine at the Barber Motorsports Museum has twin disc front brakes and is fitted with the chain drive conversion for the 750cc four devised by MV technician and team manager Arturo Magni.

MV Agusta 1973-1974 500cc

MV Agusta became a major force in GP racing from the early fifties and by 1972 factory rider Giacomo Agostini was collecting his record twelfth individual championship and the marque's 34th manufacturer's title.

Since Honda's withdrawal in 1968, MV had enjoyed some easy years in the 350cc and 500cc classes with three-cylinder four-strokes. But in the seventies a new threat loomed in the form of Yamaha and its potent water-cooled two-strokes. Yamaha's phenomenally talented Finnish rider Jaarno Saarinen beat Ago twice in the 1971 350cc championship and MV only narrowly held on to the crown in that class in 1972 by fielding a new super-agile four.

For 1973 Yamaha wheeled out its first 500cc GP bike, the water-cooled YZR500 four. Saarinen won the first two rounds on it, even though MV had countered with an enlarged 433cc version of the 350cc four and strengthened the team by signing five-times world champion Phil Read.

Things looked grim for the once mighty MV team. Agostini had failed to score points at the first two GPs and Read only had points from one second place to Saarinen. Team boss Arturo Magni had the factory working flat-out on a full 500cc four, which was ready for Read to ride in the third, German, round. The British rider won, having passed Saarinen before the Yamaha's chain failed.

Experienced and stylish Phil Read on the MV Agusta four. He won the 1973 and 1974 500cc world championships for the Italian factory, the last four-stroke title winners in grand prix racing until the MotoGP formula was introduced in 2002.

The next 500cc round at Monza was abandoned after a terrible multiple crash in the 250cc race that killed Saarinen and Italian hero Renzo Pasolini.

As the season wore on, relations became strained between Read and Agostini, who did not take to the new four and was unhappy to lose his grip on the 500cc crown he'd held for seven consecutive years. The two riders took three wins each in the last six GPs, but Read's better early-season points secured him the crown. At the end of the year Agostini made a shock announcement: he would ride Yamahas in 1974.

The 500cc four that made its debut in 1973 had MV's traditional in-line cylinders, tilted forwards at 25 degrees. Four valves in each cylinder were operated by gear-driven camshafts and set at a steep angle to aid breathing. Carburettors with 32mm bores were normally used, but alternative sizes were selected for particular circuits. Surprisingly, in view of the electronic ignition on the 350cc four, sparks were supplied from an old-style magneto driven off the crankshaft.

Various chassis alterations were implemented during the 1973 season. The team switched from drum brakes to discs, firstly with wire-spoked wheels and then with a seven-spoked cast-alloy type.

In 1974 Suzuki added to MV's worries with its 500cc XR14 disc-valve two-stroke square four. But Read, hero of the four-stroke rearguard, won the championship with new MV team-mate Franco Bonera runner-up. In 1975, however, Agostini narrowly beat Read to take Yamaha's first 500cc title. Read left MV, while Agostini returned for 1976. Given a higher-revving 500cc four in a new chassis, Ago took MV's last Grand Prix victory at that year's German GP.

Specifications

Make/Model: *1973-1974 500cc MV Agusta*

Engine type:
Air-cooled, in-line, four-cylinder dohc four-stroke.
Displacement: *499cc (58 x 47mm)*
Fuel system: *4 x 32mm Dell' Orto carburettors*
Ignition: *magneto*
Lubrication system: *wet sump*
Maximum power: *98ps @ 14,000rpm*
Maximum speed: *177mph/285km/h*

Transmission:
Gearbox: *6-speed*
Primary drive: *gears*
Clutch: *dry, multi-plate*
Final drive: *chain*

Chassis and Running Gear:
Frame type: *tubular, open-bottomed*
Front suspension: *telescopic fork*
Rear suspension: *box-section swingarm with twin shocks*
Front/rear wheels: *cast alloy 18in (wire spoked also used)*
Front/rear tyres: *Avon 110/80 x 18in/130/65 x 18in (modern fitment)*
Front brake: *Twin 280mm discs*
Rear brake: *Single 230mm disc*
Weight: *120kg (265lb)*
Fuel capacity: *18 litres*

MV's tubular frames enjoyed a reputation for superb handling.

White-faced Smiths rev-counter is retained at a time when electronic tachometers were being widely adopted.

Perforations in the front number plate let air flow through an oil cooler used on the four in 1974. Disc brakes and cast alloy wheels were a novel feature of GP bikes in the early Seventies.

John Player Norton
TX72 1972 750cc

After the Norton name changed hands in 1966, the newly formed Norton Villiers company developed and launched the 750cc Commando roadster. By 1969 Norton was fielding Commandos in production class races. Leading team rider Peter Williams, a GP-standard racer and Norton Villiers employee, became frustrated with competing on road bikes, so he persuaded the company to fund a full-on Formula 750 machine for UK events in 1971.

The results were promising and by 1972 NV's entrepreneurial boss Dennis Poore had landed the most spectacular sponsorship deal ever seen in road racing. The first proper Norton team for decades was backed by Imperial Tobacco's Number 6 cigarette brand.

Designed by Williams and other technicians at the team's base beside the Thruxton race circuit, a small batch of racers was assembled to contest the burgeoning F750 class. They were built around a tuned version of the twin-cylinder Commando engine with Quaife five-speed internals in its separate five-speed gearbox. The racing frame was a compacted version of the roadster's, even retaining the flexible engine mounts used to isolate Commando riders from the vibration typical of larger British twins.

Built low to aid handling and reduce frontal area, the TX72 had pannier fuel tanks dropping down on either side of the engine. This feature had been used by Peter Williams' father Jack when he was in charge of the AJS works team in the fifties.

Reigning 250cc world champion Phil Read races the John Player Norton on its 1972 Daytona 200 debut. Although Norton's refuelling procedures were slow compared with American teams, Read finished fourth behind Yamaha two-strokes on the 155mph Norton.

Two-into-one exhaust system terminating in a single open megaphone was replaced in mid-season by a two-pipe system.

Two-into-one exhaust system terminating in a single open megaphone was replaced in mid-season by a two-pipe system.

Pannier-style fuel tanks keep weight low. Fuel is raised to a header tank by a mechanical pump operated by the oscillation of the rear suspension's swingarm. American Union 76 stickers were applied over Shell logos as the fuel supplied for UK racing was not available at Daytona.

Roadholding and aerodynamics were vitally important. There was no time or money to develop a new engine to replace the existing 750cc ohv twin, an ancient design at the limit of its potential. The team were able to extract 70ps using track carburettors and a two-into-one exhaust devised by computer boffin Dr Gordon Blair. A prototype electronic ignition system was provided by Lucas, linked to a Krober electronic rev-counter.

The John Player team's first outing was America's early-season Daytona 200, where development rider Williams was joined by reigning 250cc world champion Phil Read. Overheating in practice was cured by discarding close-fitting air ducts around the engines and installing locally bought oil radiators in the seat fairings.

In the race, Read led for several laps and finished a creditable fourth while Williams was sidelined by gearbox failure. Engine tuning was pushing the box, originally designed to cope with less than 50ps, to breaking point.

Read was fourth again in Italy's Imola 200 race but gearbox failure was among the troubles that gave the team, now joined by John Cooper, a miserable time at the Isle of Man TT.

During 1972, a twin-pipe exhaust system was adopted, the oil cooler was moved to the fairing nose, Amal Concentric carburettors replaced the GP type and a rear hub with cush-drive was introduced. The first Player Norton team win came in August when Williams beat Paul Smart and his Imola-winning Ducati at Brands Hatch. A month later new signing Mick Grant took a win at Scarborough and Read beat Smart - now on a Kawasaki - in a triumphant Brands season finale.

Disc brake has Lockheed caliper. Carburettors are Amal GPs with remote float chambers.

Specifications

Make/Model: *John Player Norton TX72*

Engine type:
Air-cooled, twin cylinder ohv four-stroke.
Displacement: *745cc (73 x 89mm)*
Fuel system: *2 x 1 7/32in Amal GP carburettors*
Lubrication system: *dry sump*
Maximum power: *70ps @ 7,500rpm*
Maximum speed: *155mph/249km/h*

Transmission:
Gearbox: *5-speed*
Primary drive: *chain*
Clutch: *wet, multi-plate*
Final drive: *chain*

Chassis and Running Gear:
Frame type: *tubular, double cradle*
Front suspension: *telescopic fork*
Rear suspension: *swingarm with twin shocks*
Front/rear wheels: *wire spoked 19in*
Front/rear tyres: *Dunlop Racing*
Front brake: *292mm disc with AP Lockheed caliper*
Rear brake: *230mm disc with AP Lockheed caliper*
Weight: *168kg (370lb)*
Fuel capacity: *24 litres*

John Player Norton Monocoque 1973 750cc

The 1973 John Player Norton was one of the most ingenious racers ever built. Its monocoque frame not only handled superbly: it carried fuel, ducted cool air over the engine, created a carburettor airbox and provided fairing mounts.

The remarkable low-slung Norton was a direct development of the Player-sponsored team's Formula 750 machines fielded in 1972. Conceived by rider and development engineer Peter Williams, the improved machine addressed two particular shortcomings. Firstly, superlative handling, sleek aerodynamics and sure braking were needed to make up for limited power from the obsolete twin-cylinder pushrod engine. And secondly, the transmission needed beefing up.

Not the first motorcycle monocoque, but probably the earliest twin-spar frame, the structure was fabricated by Norton team technicians in stainless steel sheet. Strange as it seems today, welding aluminium presented too many technical problems at the time. The engine was moved slightly rearwards and initially, its oil reservoir was built into the frame, but a separate tank ahead of the engine was found to work better. The oil cooler was in the fairing nose as it had been in 1972.

Rear suspension was by twin Koni shocks with a braced tubular rear swingarm, while the specially made front fork featured magnesium alloy sliders. The wheels were of a cast magnesium type pioneered by Williams in the sixties, and fitted with twin disc brakes at the front and a single rotor at the rear.

John Player Norton team rider and development engineer Peter Williams at Daytona in 1973, the Monocoque's first competitive outing. His leathers and the machine's paintwork were chosen by Player to promote its No10 cigarette brand. Advertising on racing machines was new in the Seventies.

To overcome gearbox failures, a lightweight dry clutch was adopted with an extra outrigger bearing supporting its shaft, while a shock absorber was added at the chain primary drive's engine sprocket.

After a poor showing at Daytona, Williams got in the groove with three great wins in the UK's Transatlantic Trophy meetings. More glory came in the Formula 750 TT, won by Williams at a record speed of 107.27 (72.6km/h), the second fastest lap in TT history. Mick Grant was second on another monocoque.

'Willy' looked set for another high-profile win at the Silverstone International F750 race. Tucked behind the fairing, he drifted the Norton through the circuit's fast sweeping bends to lead the more powerful Suzuki two-stroke triples and break the lap record. Then, in the closing stages, he ran out of fuel. New team member Dave Croxford had led on the first lap, but his race ended in a 130mph crash. 'Crockett' was unhurt but his machine was a write-off.

Better results came with a win by Mick Grant at Scarborough and Williams scored two creditable late-season second places: behind Giacomo Agostini (500cc MV) at Mallory Park and Barry Sheene (750cc Suzuki) at Brands Hatch.

The Monocoque was dropped for 1974, the third and final year of Player sponsorship. A tubular space-frame structure with similar geometry, said to offer better accessibility to mechanics, was adopted instead. Although it suited Croxford, Williams thought it inferior to his 1973 chassis. Sadly Peter's riding career was ended abruptly when a dislodged seat unit caused him to crash heavily at Oulton Park in August 1974.

Specifications

Make/Model: *John Player Norton*

Engine type:
Air-cooled, twin-cylinder ohv four-stroke.
Displacement: *745cc (73 x 89mm)*
Fuel system: *2 x 33mm Amal Concentric carburettors*
Ignition: *Lucas RITA electronic*
Lubrication system: *dry sump*
Maximum power: *76ps @ 7,200rpm*
Maximum speed: *155mph/250km/h*

Transmission:
Gearbox: *5-speed*
Primary drive: *chain*
Clutch: *dry, multi-plate*
Final drive: *chain*

Chassis and Running Gear:
Frame type: *twin spar steel monocoque*
Front suspension: *telescopic fork*
Rear suspension: *swingarm with twin shocks*
Front/rear wheels: *five-spoke cast magnesium 18in*
Front/rear tyres: *Dunlop Racing*
Front brake: *2 x 254mm discs with AP Lockheed calipers*
Rear brake: *215mm disc with AP Lockheed caliper*
Weight: *159kg (350lb)*
Fuel capacity: *24 litres*

The fuel compartment has twin flip-up Monza filler caps for rapid refuelling. The larger is for dumping fuel in fuel while the other expels air. The Monocoque frame is fabricated from 22-guage stainless steel.

The rubber mounted oil tank is sited in the fairing ahead of the engine, as storing oil in the Monocoque caused overheating. Braced magnesium front fork sliders were made for the project

Sliding blocks on swingarm (below) are used for rear chain adjustment. Exhaust system is fixed to chassis by flexible anti-vibration mounts.

Norton NRS588
1992 588cc

Norton's victory in the 1992 Senior TT was sensational. The company's last Senior win had been in 1961 and even then its glory days in top class racing were thought to be well and truly over. But here was a bike from the historic British marque that could out-run Japan's best Superbike contenders.

Another factor made it one of history's great TT races. The Norton's rider, Steve Hislop, was locked in intense rivalry with Carl Fogarty and both men had gone to the Isle of Man determined to prove just who was the absolute master of its famous Mountain Course.

Their first clash was in the Formula 1 race. Fogarty seemed certain to win on his 750cc Loctite Yamaha when his gearbox broke. Hislop lost time misjudging his pit position on a fuel stop and despite lapping at over 123mph he had to accept second place behind first-time winner Phillip McCallen on an official Honda RC30.

In the electric Senior showdown, Hizzy and Foggy slugged it out for six record-shattering laps, the Norton rider winning by less than five seconds. His average for the 226 miles was a blistering 121.28mph.

Isle of Man Mountain course maestro Steve Hislop ends years of Japanese domination with a popular win on Norton's unorthodox Rotary in the 1992 Senior TT.

Hislop's success was all the more remarkable because the Norton ride was a hastily fixed one-off engagement. Powered by a rotary Wankel engine, the unfamiliar NRS588 had totally different characteristics from the conventional four-stroke Superbike, including a lack of engine braking effect when closing the throttle. Also, the Norton team had not had time to iron out hair-raising handling problems.

Raced under the banner of Hislop's main sponsor, the Abus lock company, the Norton was formerly part of the John Player Special team that had campaigned rotary-engined machines since 1989.

Norton had built roadgoing rotaries for police use since the early eighties and launched into racing after company employee Brian Crighton built a 170mph track prototype in 1987. The twin-rotor power unit was rated at 588cc, based on the volume of two single combustion chambers, although a Wankel engine's complete power cycle is achieved in one revolution, unlike a four-stroke piston engine's two.

Hislop's machine was the latest NRS588 version developed after Crighton left the Player-sponsored equipe run by former Honda Britain team boss Barry Symmons. For the TT, its liquid-cooled engine was modified by adding a crankshaft oil feed to cool hard-worked bearings in the core of the unit.

The aluminium chassis was designed for the JPS team by Ron Williams of suspension specialist Maxton Engineering and made by Harris Performance. The monoshock rear suspension's swingarm was beefed up to deal with the punishing Manx roads, but Hislop struggled to get a satisfactory set-up. Stiffened springing curbed terrifying weaves he experienced on the straights, but prevented the bike from remaining firmly planted when going around corners.

The Player team disbanded after 1992 and Crighton came to the fore with his version of the rotary, which won a major UK championship in 1994. But by then the Norton factory was in financial trouble and finding it impossible to produce enough machines for Superbike class homologation.

Norton's liquid-cooled twin-rotor Wankel engine delivered a healthy 140ps with masses of torque.

An especially sturdy swingarm was used for the rigours of the TT Mountain Course. The secondary pipe joining the main exhaust is an extractor to draw cool air through the engine.

The front brakes have AP Lockheed four-piston calipers made from solid billet

Specifications

Make/Model: Norton NRS588

Engine type:
Twin-rotor Wankel rotary.
Displacement: 588cc
Fuel system: 2 x 36mm Keihin flat-slide carburettors
Ignition: CDI with Hall effect triggering
Lubrication system: throttle-linked injection
Maximum power: 140ps @ 9,800rpm
Maximum speed: 190mph/290km/h

Transmission:
Gearbox: 6-speed
Primary drive: belt
Clutch: dry, multi-plate
Final drive: chain

Chassis and Running Gear:
Frame type: twin-spar aluminium
Front suspension: WP inverted telescopic fork
Rear suspension: single Maxton shock
Front/rear wheels: three-spoke PVM magnesium 17in
Front/rear tyres: Michelin radial 17in
Front brake: 2 x 310mm discs
Rear brake: 250mm drum
Weight: 310lb (140kg)
Fuel capacity: 24 litres

Rea Yamaha
1977 750cc

Joey Dunlop's victory in the 1977 Silver Jubilee TT was the first of the great Irish road racer's unrivalled total of 26 wins on the Isle of Man's Mountain Course. It was only Dunlop's second year on the difficult 37.733-mile circuit and the unkempt 25 year-old from Ballymoney was not on a factory machine, but a hybrid bike built from disparate parts.

Joey's mount was entered simply as a Yamaha, sponsored by Rea Distribution, a Larne-based transport company run by racing devotee John Rea and his brothers. Wanting a powerful Yamaha TZ750, but wary of its reputation for scary handling, Dunlop favoured the UK-made Seeley chassis on his other Rea-sponsored bikes.

A Seeley frame intended for a Suzuki engine was obtained and modified to accept a second-hand four-cylinder TZ750 engine. The unit was from a bike that had been badly mangled in a pile-up at a 1975 Brands Hatch meeting.

The rear suspension was altered, with a lengthened swingarm and re-positioned shocks to gain longer travel, as offered on the monoshock frames then being widely adopted.

Morris magnesium alloy wheels imported from America were fitted with disc brakes using Lockheed calipers with modified Yamaha rotors. A convoluted exhaust system, with one pipe crossing from the left of the engine to emerge high on the right, was based on the latest 750cc Yamaha practice. The pipes were fashioned by Mervyn 'Curly' Scott and his brother Jim, friends and racing associates of Dunlop's who did much of the fabrication work.

This is the Seeley-framed Yamaha that Joey Dunlop rode to win the Isle of Man Jubilee TT on in 1977. It also featured in the BBC documentary The Road Racers.

The 1977 Jubilee race was a one-off event, marking the TT's 70th anniversary as well as Queen Elizabeth's 25th. Sponsored by the mixer drinks brand Schweppes, it was an invitation race for machines up to 1000cc and slick tyres were prohibited.

Established TT stars Chas Mortimer, Mick Grant and Phil Read were not in the four-lap race, which Dunlop led from start to finish. On his second circuit, with a flying start and reduced fuel load, he averaged 110.93mph to make him the third fastest TT rider in history.

Excessive rear tyre wear had been a worry in practice and after experiencing some slides, Dunlop stopped 23 miles out at Parliament Square in Ramsey on the final lap and dismounted to inspect the tread. He set off again to take the chequered flag almost a minute ahead of George Fogarty (father of Nineties star Carl Fogarty), reporting that fuel leaking from the tank filler cap had affected the rear tyre.

The £1000 cash prize was the biggest Joey had collected in his racing career, but after a couple of lean years at the TT he became familiar with the victor's rostrum. His 1980 Classic TT win on a Rea Racing monoshock TZ750 gained him a place in the Honda Britain team and the quietly-spoken Ulsterman became a hugely popular TT icon who took his final three race wins in 2000, at the age of 48. Two months later Joey Dunlop was killed in a 125cc race at Tallin, Estonia.

Race bikes tend to change during their lives, just as their riders do too. This one is a classic for that, having started life as a 700cc machine. Note also the American Morris mag wheels.

A view of the once 700cc, four-cylinder, two-stroke engine, now bored out to 750cc.

Simple instrumentation is added (top), whilst a selection of exhaust pipes protrude from one side of the machine, next to the modified Seeley frame.

Specifications

Make/Model: 750cc Rea Yamaha

Engine type:
Water-cooled, in-line four piston-port two-stroke.
Displacement: 747cc (66 x 54mm)
Fuel system: 4 x 34mm Mikuni carburettors
Ignition: CDI magneto
Lubrication system: petroil
Maximum power: 130ps @ 11,000rpm (estimated)
Maximum speed: 175mph/282km/h (dependent on gearing)

Transmission:
Gearbox: 6-speed
Primary drive: gears
Clutch: dry, multi-plate
Final drive: chain

Chassis and Running Gear:
Frame type: tubular, double cradle
Front suspension: telescopic fork
Rear suspension: tubular swingarm with twin shocks
Front/rear wheels: wire-spoked type 18in
Front/rear tyres: Dunlop KR1243.50 x 18in/KR111 3.50 x 18in
Front brake: twin disc
Rear brake: 2 discs with Lockheed calipers
Weight: n/a
Fuel capacity: 25 litres

Suzuki XR34 1980

With Barry Sheene riding Yamahas for 1980 and having taken a big chunk of sponsorship with him, Heron Suzuki almost quit GPs. But instead they decided to contest the season with the XR34 square-four two-stroke. If they were serious about beating the likes of Sheene and Roberts they needed some talented riders. They employed rising American star Randy Mamola, perhaps the greatest rider of the era not to win the world title, and New Zealander Graeme Crosby. Two other teams contested the 500GP series with XR34s. The Italian Olio Nava Fiat Team fielded Marco Lucchinelli and Graziano Rossi, father of the legendary Valentino. Another team, Riemersma-Nimag, had Dutch ace Wil Hartog.

The 1980 season got off to a slow start when snow cancelled the Austrian opener at the Salzburgring. The first round therefore was Italy where Lucchinelli netted pole and Mamola was third on the grid behind Roberts. But in the race itself, four of the Suzukis retired. Mamola, Lucchinelli and Hartog all suffered main bearing failure while Crosby's bike seized. Rossi managed third and Yamaha's Kenny Roberts was the race winner.

The Italian teams favoured 16in wheels for which only Michelin produced tyres. The British team used 18in wheels which afforded a wider tyre choice.

The next round was Spain where Mamola, Rossi and Hartog stuck with the new XR34M while Crosby and Lucchinelli went with the older tried and tested XR34H. Hartog opted for the older bike too and gave his XR34M chassis to Mamola. Lucchinelli and Mamola were second and third to Roberts. Crosby was a distant twelfth while Rossi and Hartog both crashed.

Things were starting to improve for Suzuki in the French GP at Paul Ricard, and Lucchinelli and Mamola diced hard with Roberts. But Roberts won again, followed home by Mamola, Lucchinelli, Rossi and Crosby.

Talented New Zealand racer Graeme Crosby lifts off as he tackles the 1980 Isle of Man TT.
He went onto win the race at an average speed of 109.65 mph (175.44kph).

Side-mounted 36mm Mikuni racing carb is one of four feeding the thirsty two-stroke. Its spindly chassis and big power for the time make the heroics of the riders all the more sensational, none more so than Graeme Crosby's 1980 Senior TT win.

Perhaps the finest hour for the XR34H came at the Isle of Man Senior TT. Graeme Crosby won the event with an average speed for the race of 109.65mph.

At Assen for the Dutch TT round of the GP series Mamola was the early leader, but visor misting problems in the damp conditions caused him to slow, the same problem he'd had at Paul Ricard. Lucchinelli suffered visor difficulties too, eventually losing his completely. Yamaha's Jack Middelburg was the eventual winner with Rossi third and Mamola fifth.

Things finally came good in the Belgian GP at Zolder with Mamola taking the win with Lucchinelli second, Roberts third and Crosby and Hartog following them home.

Mamola was 12 points behind Roberts going into the Finnish GP and needed the win to keep his title hopes alive. Lucchinelli retired with a fuel leak while Rossi retired with a blown head gasket. Hartog won and Mamola was fourth, hampered by a wrist injury from a practice crash.

At Silverstone Mamola was the race winner with Lucchinelli third and Rossi fourth. Hartog retired and a puncture put Crosby in 13th place.

In the final round at the Nurburgring Lucchinelli won from Crosby and Hartog. Mamola was fifth while Rossi retired. Their combined efforts in that season were enough to net Suzuki its fifth successive manufacturer's title while Mamola and Lucchinelli were second and third in the riders' standings behind Roberts.

Make/Model: *Suzuki XR34*

Engine type:
Liquid-cooled, square-four two-stroke.
Displacement: *494.69cc (54 x 54mm)*
Fuel system: *4 x 36mm Mikuni VM36SS
carburettors*
Ignition: *electronic*
Lubrication system: *two-stroke*
Maximum power: *125bhp @ 10,800rpm*
Maximum speed: *191mph*

Transmission:
Gearbox: *6-speed*
Primary drive: *gear*
Clutch: *dry, multi-plate*
Final drive: *chain*

Chassis and Running Gear:
Frame type: *duplex tubular cradle*
Front suspension: *Kayaba
telescopic fork*
Rear suspension: *swingarm with twin
Girling shocks*
Front/rear wheels: *18in (16in for
Italian teams)*
Front/rear tyres: *2.50/4.00*
Front brake: *twin floating 310mm discs*
Rear brake: *220mm disc*
Weight: *144kg (dry)*
Fuel capacity: *Regulation*

*Kayaba front forks are pneumatically assisted. Opposed
pistons on each caliper can be bled separately for maximum
braking efficiency.*

Suzuki XR23B 1979 500cc

Suzuki had started development of the XR23 as early as 1976, and its most famous riders would be the entertaining double act of Steve Parrish and Barry Sheene in the MCN Superbike Championship in 1979. The XR23, better known as the RG700, was built as a large capacity version of the RG500 and was originally conceived as a development mule for components for the 500cc GP bikes. The bike displaced 652cc and this was achieved by raising the 500's bore from 54 to 62mm making it hugely oversquare, yielding extremely high power. In fact, so powerful was it that the early versions had to be tuned down to 135bhp.

Two XR23 innovations that were used on the GP bikes, firstly on the 1978 XR22, were stepped barrels on the square-four two-stroke motor and a cassette type gearbox. The first of these made for better engine cooling and lowered the centre of gravity to improve handling, while the second allowed quick and easy gearbox changes so that different ratios could be tried out at different circuits.

The XR23B arrived in 1978 and is easy to spot with its wider tail unit. This had to be the size it is to accommodate the large expansion chambers that a large-capacity two-stroke demands. As the rule book did not permit pipes that extended beyond the back wheel, the chambers for the rear cylinder had to be wider and curved and housed under the seat. The front ones were large too and the result was that the XR23's rider would get a hot backside and feet. Barry Sheene answered these problems by reverting to earlier pipes, gaining comfort at the loss of some top-end power.

Although used by Barry Sheene and several other riders, this was also the machine that Pat Hennen broke the twenty-minute barrier at the Isle of Man. It was initially built to race in the 750 formula and at Daytona.

Sheene was a fan of the bike but the other riders – Parrish, Pat Hennen, Tom Herron and Wil Hartog – were less keen. Parrish and Herron both broke their collarbones falling from the bike at Donington with a few seconds of each other.

Suspension was of the highest order for the day, with Kayaba nitrogen-charged anti-dive forks up front and a nitrogen-filled, fully adjustable shock at the rear, but still the handling posed problems. With an extremely short wheelbase and huge power for the day, the XR23 would wheelie everywhere in the first four gears. Parrish was the first to cure that by strapping a weight above the front exhausts, much to the disgust of Suzuki themselves. Sheene cottoned on to this, and after regularly stealing Parrish's one, had his own made. The Japanese also turned their noses up at Sheene's use of the old-type power-sapping exhausts, but as Sheene felt that the bike had too much power anyway, he wasn't to be discouraged.

In the UK-based 1979 MCN Superbike Championship, Parrish was fifth overall and Sheene sixth. The bike was raced only a handful of times the following year.

Specifications

Make/Model: *Suzuki XR23*

Engine type:
Liquid-cooled, square-four two-stroke.
Displacement: *498.7cc (62.6 x 54mm)*
Fuel system: *4 x 36mm Mikuni VM36SS carburettors*
Ignition system: *electronic*
Lubrication system: *two-stroke*
Maximum power: *138bhp @ 10,800rpm*
Maximum speed: *191mph*

Transmission:
Gearbox: *6-speed*
Primary drive: *gears*
Clutch: *dry, multi-plate*
Final drive: *chain*

Chassis and Running Gear:
Frame type: *twin loop tubular cradle*
Front suspension: *Kayaba pneumatic telescopic fork*
Rear suspension: *aluminium swingarm with Kayaba monoshock*
Front/rear wheels: *16in carbon/magnesium composite*
Front/rear tyres: *Michelin 3.50/4.00*
Front brake: *2 x 310mm discs*
Rear brake: *230mm disc*
Weight: *136kg (dry)*
Fuel capacity: *NA*

Long stingers (top) fight the uneven battle of silencing the exhaust emissions from the front two cylinders. Bulbous tail unit contains the rear cylinders' expansion chambers. Despite a chunky steering damper (left), the XR23B was a fearsome handler.

With the fairing lowers removed the XR's side-mounted carbs are plainly visible as are the four pick-ups for the ignition (above). Breather ahead of the fuel cap (below) is essential to prevent the quickly drained tank from forming a vacuum lock.

Suzuki XR69-S/GS 1000R 1981-82 1000cc

The British press called him 'win-a-week Marshall'. Throughout the 1982 season, Roger Marshall won race after race on this Team Texaco Heron Suzuki GB four-stroke, beating some of the biggest stars of the day. He finished the year as UK Formula One champion and was voted Man of the Year by the readers of the weekly Motor Cycle News.

Marshall's machine was one of the 998cc XR69 in-line fours supplied by the factory for the Suzuki GB team to field in the flourishing TT Formula One class. The category had been inaugurated as part of the great Isle of Man TT shake-up after the event lost FIM Grand Prix status in 1977. Carrying FIM world championship status, it was open to 601cc-1000cc four-strokes and 351cc-500cc two-strokes based on volume production models.

Also called the GS1000R, the X69 derived from Suzuki's GS1000 roadster launched for 1978. Factory race development was focused on 500cc two-strokes at the time, so veteran tuner 'Pops' Yoshimura was entrusted with tuning the two-valves-per-cylinder double overhead camshaft engine. The chassis featured a tubular steel double cradle frame with sophisticated suspension transferred from the 500cc Grand Prix programme, including front forks with anti-dive.

The first version raced in 1980 with instant success. New Zealand's Graeme Crosby, in his first year with Suzuki, took the growling one-litre four to wins in the Daytona 100-mile Superbike race, the Australian Swann Series and, with American co-rider Wes Cooley, in Japan's Suzuka 8 Hour race. He finished second to Mick Grant's Honda in the Formula One TT, but his win in the Ulster GP round secured the overall 1980 individual championship and the manufacturer's title for Suzuki.

The first version of the 1000cc machine raced in 1980 and was an instant success in the hands of New Zealander Graeme Crosby. Later machines such as this 1981 version were also winners in the capable hands of Roger Marshall and of course Crosby.

An updated XR69-S, featuring Full Floater monoshock rear suspension developed for the GP team's 500cc two-strokes, was raced in 1981. Croz won at Daytona again and went on to scoop the Formula One TT as well as the championship.

Intense rivalry between Suzuki and Honda helped make the 1981 Formula One one of the most controversial races in TT history. On the Isle of Man course, riders set off at timed intervals and replacing a rear wheel with a flat tyre caused Croz to miss his slot. He started from the back of the field and rode a blinding race, breaking the class lap record and finishing in third position. After deliberation, the organisers credited Croz with the lost time and declared him the race winner.

The furious Honda team boss made a gesture of protest by fielding black-painted machines and riders in black leathers in the 1000cc Classic finale a few days later. But Crosby won convincingly and his XR69-S team-mate Mick Grant was second.

When he first rode the XR69-S, Roger Marshall fell foul of its propensity to bend valves whenever a gear selection in the five-speed box was missed. But he soon got the hang of the mighty Suzuki and the top riders he beat on it included Honda-mounted Ron Haslam, Wayne Gardner and Joey Dunlop.

The XR69 can be easily identified from the other machines of the period. The bodywork at the rear is unique as is the way the exhaust/silencer is positioned.

A view under the fuel tank of the XR69 reveals the carburettors and their trumpet style intakes.

Not the normal silencer system, this is short and stubby but worked well all the same (top). Twin discs and calipers for the front brake setup (bottom).

Specifications

Make/Model: *Suzuki XR69-S*

Engine type:
Air-cooled, in-line, four-cylinder dohc four-stroke.
Displacement: *998cc*
Fuel system: *4 x 29mm Keihin carburettors*
Ignition: *Nippon-Denso CDI*
Lubrication system: *wet sump*
Maximum power: *134ps @ 9,500rpm*
Maximum speed: *189mph/305 km/h*

Transmission:
Gearbox: *5-speed*
Primary drive: *gear*
Clutch: *wet, multi-plate*
Final drive: *chain*

Chassis and Running Gear:
Frame type: *tubular double cradle*
Front suspension: *Kayaba telescopic fork*
Rear suspension: *Full Floater with Kayaba shock*
Front/rear wheels: *Dymag three-spoked 18in*
Front/rear tyres: *Dunlop /170/160 x 18in*
Front brake: *Twin 310mm floating discs*
Rear brake: *Single 240mm disc*
Weight: *159kg (350lb)*
Fuel capacity: *24 litres*

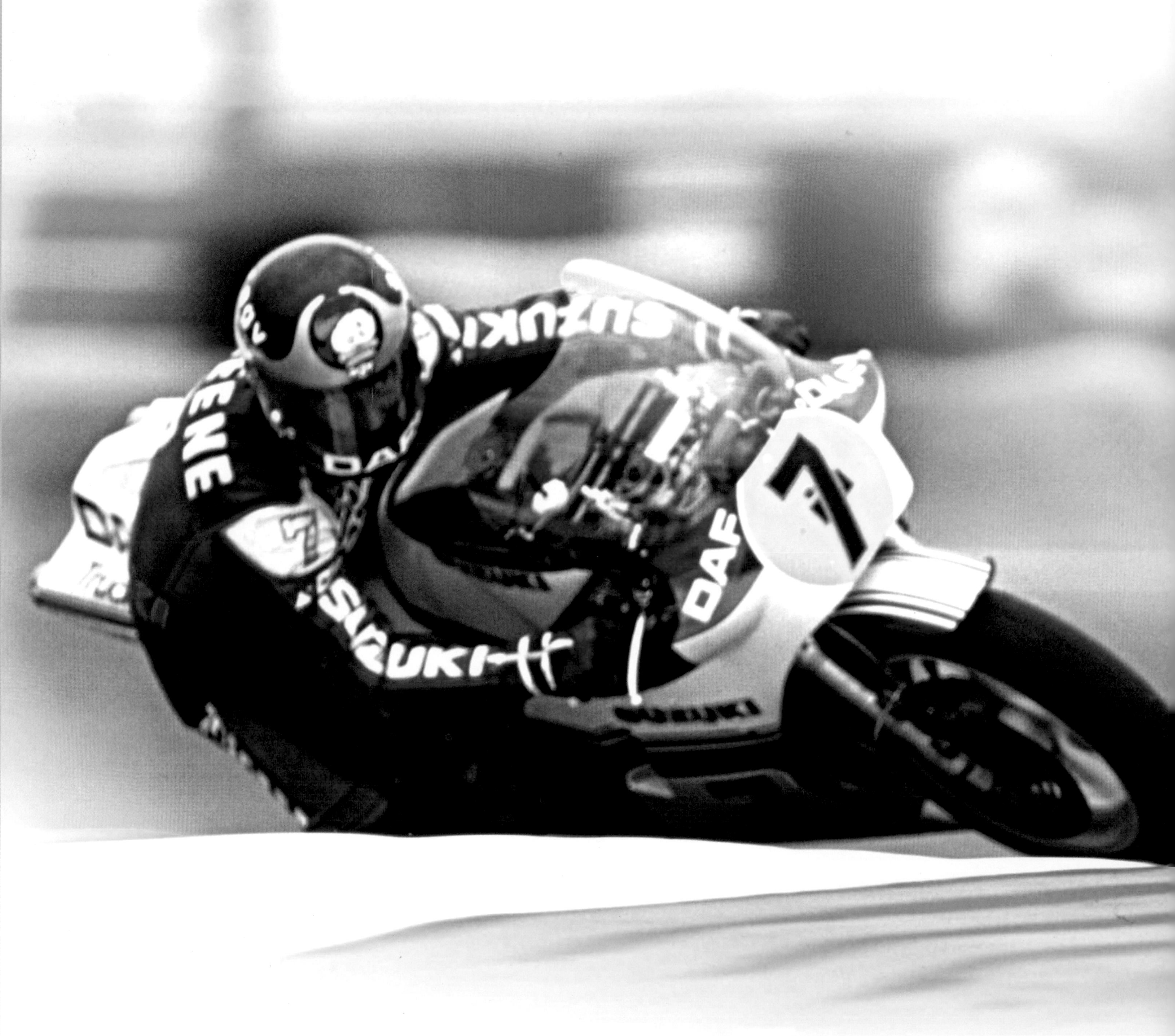
SUZUKI
DAF
7
DAF

Suzuki XR45 1984

Suzuki's XR45 was the machine on which Barry Sheene would take his last-ever GP podium in his farewell 1984 season.

By Sheene's valedictory year the square-four two-stroke Suzuki was outclassed and outpowered by the V4 Hondas and Yamahas. But that didn't stop him from delivering some spirited performances, his best finish being a plucky third in the opening round at a very wet Kyalami, South Africa.

Sheene began his 500GP career with Suzuki GB in 1973, going on to win back-to-back championships in 1976 and 1977, elevating himself to become the most famous British motorcycle racer ever.

However Sheene was frustrated by Suzuki's slow development and set up his own team to race leased Yamahas for 1980. But ultimately his privateer team's machines (some factory support came eventually) lacked the outright pace of the full works bikes and he returned to Suzuki GB for 1983. That was a slow

year for Sheene as he was still recovering from injuries sustained in the Silverstone crash that nearly killed him the previous season. At the time of the 1982 accident he was equal on points with his arch rival, Yamaha's Kenny Roberts. Despite missing the last five races of the '82 season he still finished fifth overall.

For 1984 Sheene had two XR45s, one a factory bike and the other featuring a Harris Performance Products aluminium frame. The British firm made the chassis so that the steering geometry could be altered by adjusting the head angle to suit different circuits. Harris also developed adjustable rear suspension to allow Sheene to make the most of what power was available and get the best from the tyres. Michelin were no longer providing Sheene with their very best tyres and this only served to compound the problems. Suzuki didn't develop a V4 to compete directly with the Honda and Yamaha.

Racing legend Barry Sheene at full speed on his DAF sponsored XR45. This was taken at the Silverstone Grand Prix of 1984.

Number 7, one of the most iconic in the history of motorcycle racing, was campaigned at the top level by Barry Sheene for the last time in 1984 on the Suzuki XR45. With an obsolete engine he had to ride beyond the bike just to stay with the front-runners. Harris Performance developed a chassis to allow variable steering geometry and rear suspension.

Although Suzuki had modified the square-four motor in the decade it had been using the layout, the configuration was at the end of its developmental line. Even though Italian Franco Uncini won the 1982 series for Suzuki, Yamaha and then Honda overhauled them in subsequent years. Effectively Sheene and the team were on their own. It would be 1988 before Suzuki would make a full-time works return to 500GPs.

Rumours of Sheene's impending retirement were rife in 1984, but although he would retire it wasn't totally out of choice. And it wasn't in his character to go out with a whimper. Following his brilliant third and what would turn out to be his last podium at Kyalami, Sheene rode his XR45 on the limit, running in second place in races on occasion, struggling to keep superior machinery at bay before being thwarted more than once by mechanical failure or handling problems.

The XR was still competitive at a domestic level, however, and the final race win of Sheene's full-time career (he took up classic racing in the late 90s and won) came at Scarborough's Oliver's Mount in 1984 in the two-leg Gold Cup, Sheene winning the second race.

Sheene's top-flight career ended at Donington at the end of 1984. He had hoped to compete in 1985 but with Suzuki having withdrawn from GPs he was unable to secure a top-level ride elsewhere.

Once again, large expansion chambers demand a bulbous tail unit. Square four layout (bottom) was old news in 1984 as the top machines had move to V4.

Specifications

Make/Model: *Suzuki XR45*

Engine type:
Liquid-cooled, square-four two-stroke.
Displacement: *498cc (56 x 50.6mm)*
Fuel system: *4 x 36mm or 38mm cylindrical Mikuni carburettors*
Ignition: *electronic*
Lubrication system: *two-stroke*
Maximum power: *135 - 140ps @11000rpm variable*
Maximum speed: *N/A*

Transmission:
Gearbox: *6-speed, various ratios available*
Primary drive: *gear*
Clutch: *dry, multi-plate*
Final drive: *chain*

Chassis and Running Gear:
Frame type: *twin loop square-section aluminium tubing*
Front suspension: *Kayaba telescopic fork*
Rear suspension: *swingarm with Kyaba monoshock*
Front/rear wheels: *16in Campagnola*
Front/rear tyres: *Michelin 3.50/4.50*
Front brake: *2 x 300mm steel discs*
Rear brake: *220mm cast iron disc*
Weight: *NA*
Fuel capacity: *NA*

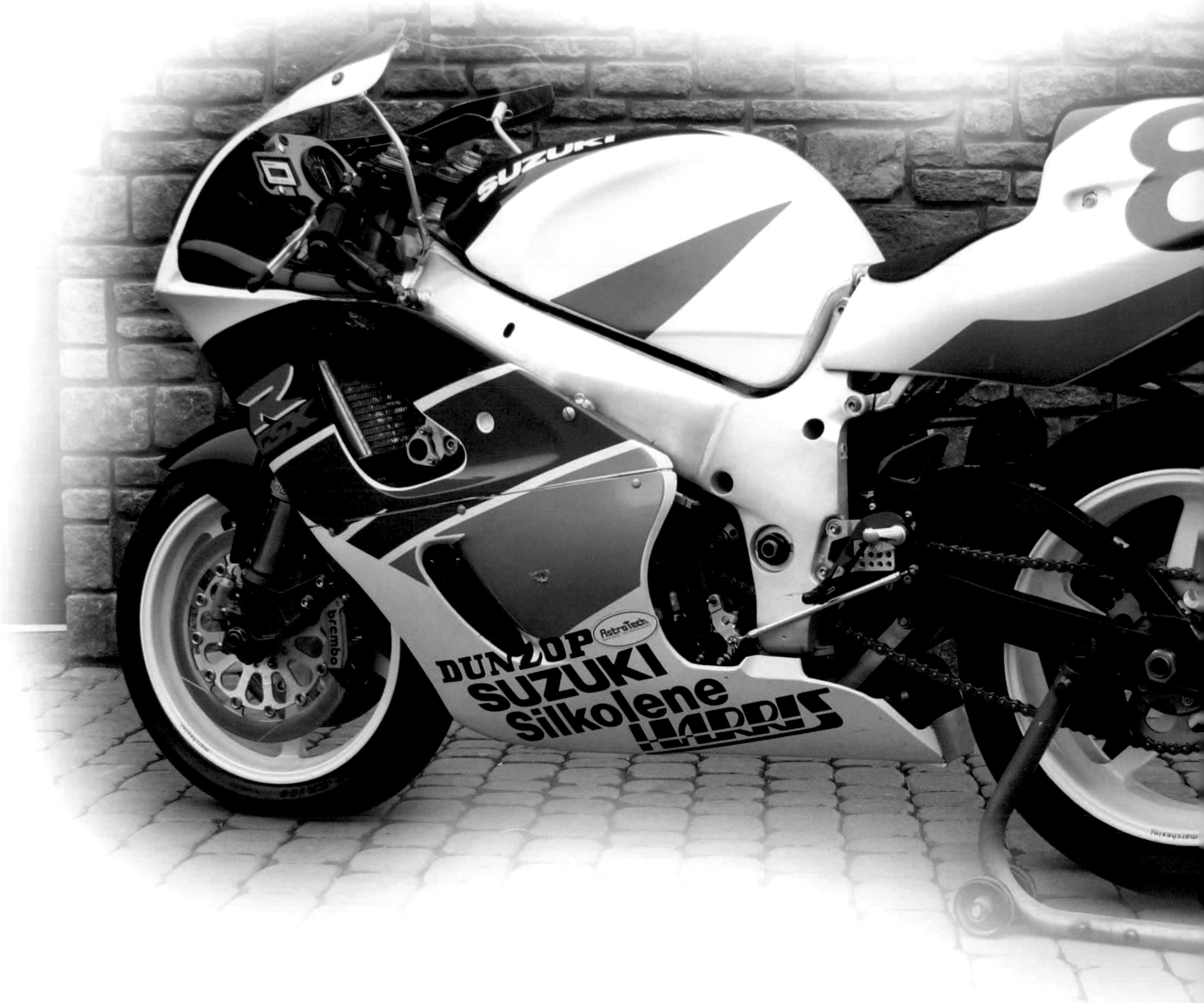
SUZUKI
SUZUKI
Silkolene
brembo

Suzuki GSX-R750 World Superbike 1998

This is the machine that British ace Jamie Whitham had a tumultuous season on in World Superbikes in 1998. By then the GSX-R750 was long-established and die-hard fans of the light and powerful road bikes were praying for competition success. Suzuki had launched a new version of the GSX-R750 with fuel injection replacing carburettors for 1998. But it would be up against some stiff competition in WSB, with the 750cc four-cylinder bike giving away 250cc to the Ducati twins.

The year didn't get off to the best of starts for Whitham and the Harris Suzuki team. He crashed at 150mph at Eastern Creek in testing when the throttle jammed open, writing the bike off but walking away unscathed. The Nippon Denso fuel injection proved problematic too. Whitham remembers: 'We never did get it right, it was a shame we were tied in to Nippon Denso and couldn't go elsewhere. I ended up using carburettors for all the races.'

There were handling problems too and Whitham and team-mate Peter Goddard tried a variety of swingarms and suspension linkages to combat the problem. Says Whitham: 'With most bikes you can find a benchmark within three or four days of testing and that base setting just needs tweaking at different tracks. But the Suzuki was like a different bike at every circuit. Every weekend it felt like we were starting the season all over again.'

As much as Jamie Whitham and Peter Goddard tried during the 1998 Superbike series, success was not really theirs to have. The competition was strong, in particular the Ducati's, and so the Suzuki GSX-R750 struggled to keep up.

There was no arguing with the GSX-R750's race kit brakes (left) with their cast-iron rotors and Brembo calipers. Forks are full factory as supplied to the Harris Team.
WSB bike (below) retains silhouette of the road bike, but there was a lot more than that going on under the fairing.

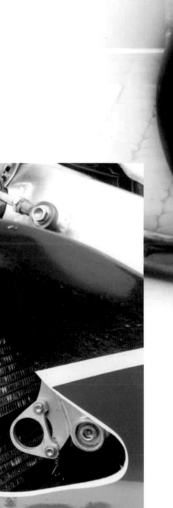

Whitham also remembers that while the bikes made good top end power, by his reckoning around 165bhp, the bikes lacked the mid-range punch so crucial to getting good drive out of corners. 'The Japanese were constantly providing us with different camshafts to try and get the mid-range back,' remembers Whitham.

The problems were reflected in the results too. Early on in the season Whitham's best placing was fifth in Monza, Italy. Peter Goddard made fourth in the second race of the season opener in Australia. But the team's persistence paid off a little by mid-season with Whitham taking the bike's best result that season, third in the second race of the Brands Hatch round. Now that he was posting more consistent results, Whitham was confident that Suzuki would want to retain his services for the following season. 'But they didn't want me. I knew that the deal between Harris and Suzuki was about to end its three-year term and Alstare Corona were taking over, but I thought they'd want to keep me after all the development I'd done,' he says. In the end Suzuki employed Pierfrancesco Chili and Katsuaki Fujiwara.

But Whitham was able to take some credit for Keiichi Kitigawa's win at Sugo in 1998, as the Japanese used chassis settings that Whitham had worked out for his own GSX-R750.

Real-time lap timer sits to the left of the rev counter (top). Swingarm and shock linkages were frequently changed in pursuit of traction and handling.

Specifications

Make/Model: *Suzuki GSX-R750 WSB bike*

Engine type:
Liquid-cooled, inline-four four-stroke.
Displacement: *749cc (72 x 46mm)*
Fuel system: *4 x various size Mikuni flatslides*
Ignition: *electronic ignition*
Lubrication system: *wet sump*
Maximum power: *165bhp @ 14,00rpm*
Maximum speed: *190mph (est)*

Transmission:
Gearbox: *6-speed*
Primary drive: *gears*
Clutch: *multi-plate*
Final drive: *chain*

Chassis and Running Gear:
Frame type: *twin-spar aluminium*
Front suspension: *telescopic fork, adj. preload, rebound and compression damping*
Rear suspension: *monoshock adj. preload, rebound and compression damping*
Front/rear wheels: *17in*
Front/rear tyres: *120/70 190/50*
Front brake: *2 x 320 discs*
Rear brake: *single 220mm*
Weight: *162kg*
Fuel capacity: *18 litres*

Triumph T150 Trident
1970-1975 750cc

Riders and race fans loved Slippery Sam. Comfortable, controllable and dependable, Sam cruised to five consecutive Production TT race wins, including one over 10 laps of the Isle of Man's 37.73-mile Mountain Course. For many British fans watching, victories by a Triumph boosted morale at a time when the home industry was sliding into terminal crisis.

Sam was a 750cc Triumph Trident built for Production class racing at the factory in 1970. Class rules of the time allowed clip-on handlebars, single seats, large capacity fuel tanks and non-standard brakes. Permitted engine tuning boosted output from the stock 59ps up to 75ps with standard silencers in place and a Quaife five-speed gearbox cluster listed as an optional extra was fitted.

Factory Tridents finished first and fourth in the 1970 750cc Production TT and it was the second one home which earned its nickname later in the season. Competing in France's Bol d'Or 24-hour endurance race, it was afflicted by a scavenging problem in the lubrication system. Much of the machine was covered in oil, as were the leathers of riders Percy Tait and Steve Jolly. They still managed to finish fifth, but it was a slippery experience!

Ray Pickrell racing the factory Production Trident in its original form with a Fontana drum front brake. The standard 'ray gun' silencers, raised to gain cornering clearance, were efficient and did not reduce power by much.

For 1971 factory Tridents were modified by fitting a subtly altered frame, which gave a useful increase in cornering clearance. Sam was allotted to team rider Ray Pickrell for the Production TTs of 1971 and 1972, winning both at 100mph-plus average speed to beat Norton and BMW twins.

When financial crisis hit the BSA Group that owned Triumph, racing activity had to be curtailed. Sam's 1972 TT entry was only agreed at the last minute, when mechanic Fred Swift rode the machine from the factory in Warwickshire to the Isle of Man ferry terminal in Liverpool. At the end of the season, former team manager Les Williams bought Sam from the company.

To maintain the bike's competitive edge Williams had a new frame built in lightweight Renolds 531 tube. Ex-Triumph team rider Tony Jefferies rode Sam through hail and sleet to a third TT win in 1973. Later that year Triumph employee Percy Tait won a Silverstone Production race on Sam, setting a class lap record of 103.31mph.

Further updating for 1974 saw the 250mm Fontana drum front brake replaced by twin discs and the latest Quaife gearbox internals were installed. Mick Grant rode Sam to TT victory number four, despite having his right wrist in plaster and racing against bigger machines allowed by the class limit being changed from 750cc to 1000cc.

For the 1975 ten-lap TT, Triumph's new owner Norton Villiers Triumph (NVT) supported Sam's entry, so the bike was repainted in the red, white and black Norton team colours. In the 377-mile marathon teams of two riders took turns to circulate and Sam's winning pilots were rising star Alex George and seasoned Dave Croxford of the NVT race team.

After that Sam was retired, simply because Production class rules barred machines more than five years old.

Make/Model: *Triumph 150 Trident*

Engine type:
Air-cooled, in-line, three-cylinder ohv four-stroke.
Displacement: *741cc (67 x 70mm)*
Fuel system: *3 x 27mm Amal carburettors*
Ignition: *3 x coils with points*
Lubrication system: *dry sump*
Maximum power: *75ps*
Maximum speed: *320 km/h*

Transmission:
Gearbox: *5-speed*
Primary drive: *chain*
Clutch: *dry, single plate*
Final drive: *chain*

Chassis and Running Gear:
Frame type: *tubular, Renolds 531*
Front suspension: *telescopic fork*
Rear suspension: *swingarm with twin Girling shocks*
Front/rear wheels: *spoked 19in*
Front/rear tyres: *DunlopTT100 4.10 x 19in /4.10 x 19in*
Front brake: *Twin 320mm discs with Lockheed calipers*
Rear brake: *2Single 220mm disc with Lockheed caliper*
Weight: *185kg (410lb)*
Fuel capacity: *23litres*

Internal engine tweaks raised power output from the Trident's standard 58ps at 7,250rpm to 74ps at 7,500rpm .

Triumph 750 triple
1971

Nineteen seventy-one was a tremendous year for the BSA/Triumph team's 750cc triples. They howled to victory in America's biggest races, the Daytona 200 and the Ontario Classic. They won the inaugural Formula 750 TT, France's Bol d'Or endurance race, a series of premier events on UK short circuits and scooped the Motor Cycle News Superbike series.

At Daytona, the team delivered a convincing 1-2-3. The winner was Dick Mann, who had won the race for Honda in 1970. Second place was taken by Triumph West Coast rider and reigning US Grand National champion Gene Romero. Both were on new 1971 triples, while fellow Californian Don Emde was third on a year-old BSA. Britain's Paul Smart had started on pole and led the race until his 1971 Triumph blew a piston after covering 160 of the 200 miles.

The latest triples were easily identified by 'letter box' air intakes at the front of their fairings. A revised, lower frame with altered steering geometry necessitated relocating the oil cooler from its old position inside the frame loop to lie horizontally inside a duct behind the intake slot. Another 1971 change was a new front end with shorter fork legs and twin disc brakes.

Gene Romero at Daytona in 1971, carrying the US champion's Number 1 plate and riding at up to 165mph without gloves. Designed with the help of a high-speed wind tunnel, the fairing included a large seat tail that was beneficial on the Florida track's flat-out banked sections.

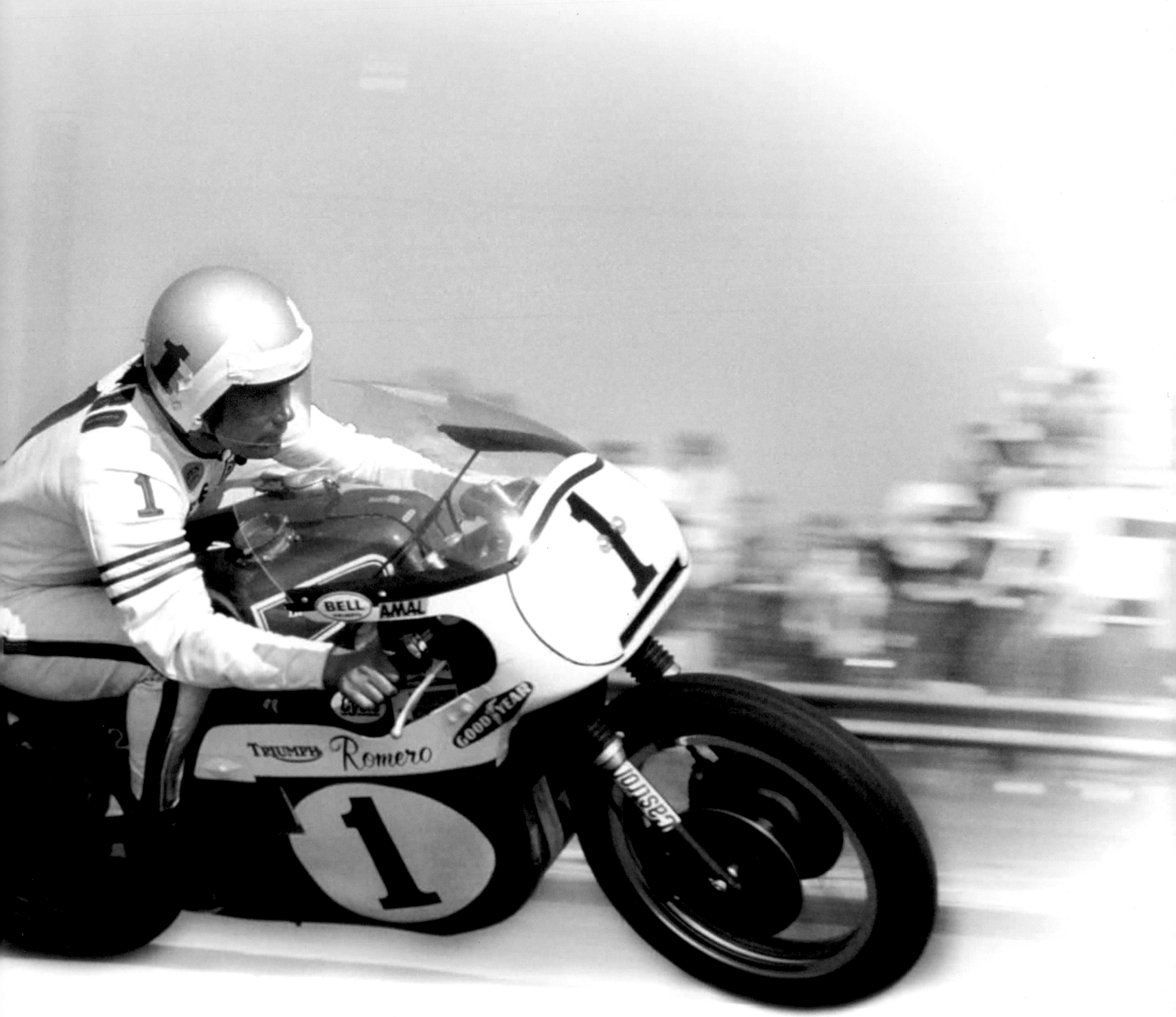
BELL
AMAL
GOOD YEAR
TRIUMPH
Romero
1

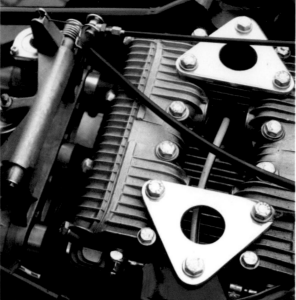

Rockers for pushrod valve gear are under finned covers. A single beam mechanism opens all three throttles.

Experimental coated aluminium discs proved troublesome due to heat expansion and were soon replaced by conventional iron rotors.

All 1971 bikes except Mann's had Amal Concentric road carburettors. Easier to tune than the GP type, they were found to give even performance throughout the rpm range. To speed up fuel stops, aircraft dry break valves were fitted on the tanks, with normal flip-up caps alongside them to let air escape while filling.

The latest engines had combustion chambers with peripheral squish bands to promote gas swirl, found to be worth an extra 2ps. Redesigned valve-operating rocker gear in some units was introduced mainly to achieve greater reliability at high rpm.

On some bikes, though not Romero's, a lightweight primary drive was fitted, with a compact multi-plate clutch in place of the standard Borg & Beck single-plate item and a lightweight magnesium oil bath casing.

Most riders who raced the British triples loved their stability and manageability as well as the strong top-end power. Romero, who was as proficient racing on dirt tracks as on asphalt, was no exception and he confessed that he also liked the blaring howl from his Triumph's three-into-one exhaust at full throttle.

BSA/Triumph's free-spending campaign in the US halted at the end of 1971. The BSA group, once one of the UK's biggest dollar earners, hit financial trouble during that year and development tailed off.

But, as Doug Hele himself acknowledged, the all-conquering triples' days looked numbered anyway. Their main rivals were Kawasaki, Suzuki and Yamaha who were rapidly developing a new breed of large capacity racing two-strokes that would take 750cc racing to a new level.

Romero moved up to that level successfully. He joined Yamaha to ride its bold new TZ750 four in 1974 and won Daytona in 1975.

Specifications

Make/Model: *Triumph 750 triple*

Engine type:
*Air-cooled, in-line, three-cylinder ohv
four-stroke.*
Displacement: *741cc (67 x 70mm)*
Fuel system: *3 x 27mm Amal Concentric
carburettors*
Ignition: *alternator and coils with points*
Lubrication system: *dry sump*
Maximum power: *85ps @ 8,200rpm*
Maximum speed: *165mph/320 km/h*

Transmission:
Gearbox: *5-speed*
Primary drive: *chain*
Clutch: *dry, single plate*
Final drive: *chain*

Chassis and Running Gear:
Frame type: *tubular, T45 tube*
Front suspension: *telescopic fork*
Rear suspension: *swingarm with twin
Girling shocks*
Front/rear wheels: *spoked 19in*
Front/rear tyres: *Dunlop KR76 3 x
19in/KR73 3.50 x 19in*
Front brake: *Twin 254mm discs with AP
Lockheed calipers*
Rear brake: *254mm disc with AP
Lockheed caliper*
Weight: *172kg (380lb)*
Fuel capacity: *25 litres*

Where the spine-tingling howl comes out at 8,000rpm: the three-into-one exhaust system's open megaphone.

Yamaha TZ750 1975

By the early 70s, Yamaha realised that the future of large-capacity road bikes lay with four-strokes because of increasingly stringent emissions regulations. Throughout the 60s they had built some brilliant two-strokes and would continue to do so for smaller capacity road bikes right into the 70s. But their large-capacity four-stroke policy gave them a problem. Race wins were vital for sales success, especially in the important American market where production bike racing had a huge following particularly in the F750 class. A big four-stroke would not be able to compete with the production-based Suzuki and Kawasaki 750cc two-stroke triples.

Yamaha's solution was to build a two-stroke four-cylinder bike. It wasn't based on any road-going machine, but the FIM granted it dispensation to race provided at least 200 were built for homologation purposes. The company announced that it would field the TZ750 in Europe and the US in 1973, but the project was delayed because of other racing commitments and the TZ didn't appear until 1974.

The bore and stroke were the same as the TZ350 twin-cylinder race bike giving the four a displacement of 694cc, although very few parts were common to both engines. It made 90bhp. After the first few hundred bikes had been built, Yamaha upped the bore to 66.4mm to take the capacity up to 747cc.

Gene Romero is congratulated by his father in the winners' enclosure after winning the 1975 Daytona 200 on a twin-shock TZ750 against more sophisticated monoshock bikes ridden by GP World Champion rivals. Sunblock under his eyes alleviate distractions and blinding from the Florida sun.

YAMAHA TZ750

Twin shocks (left) should have placed Romero at a disadvantage against the new monoshock bikes, but Romero gave the twin shock bike an epic factory-beating victory.

Giacomo Agostini won the 1974 Daytona 200 on a TZ750 on his Yamaha debut. There were around 50 entrants on TZ750s for that race and they dominated the results. An FIM sub-committee than decided that the TZ wasn't legal after all for F750 and banned it for the rest of the season. Some race organisers got round the ban by running 'open class' events. At the Imola 200 in Italy, Ago won from Kenny Roberts, also on a Yamaha, and TZ750s took all of the first four places.

The TZ750 notched up countless race successes, especially in the US with Kel Carruthers' team of Roberts, Gene Romero and Don Castro.

For 1975 the FIM ban was lifted. Romero won the 1975 Daytona 200 on a twin-shock TZ750. By that year Yamaha had developed a monoshock version of the TZ750 to counter high-speed instability that some riders had complained of. The clutch on Kenny Roberts monoshock bike failed a few laps in. Steve Baker brought the first monoshock bike home in second place while carburation problems forced Ago into fourth behind Johnny Cecotto, on a twin-shock like Romero.

Romero competed in his first Daytona in 1967 and had come close to victory in 1970 and 1971. In the 1975 race he spent most of the race in fourth before coming through the pack to put pressure on race leader Steve McLaughlin who subsequently crashed.

Yamaha TZ750s filled the first 16 places in the results.

At that year's Imola, Johnny Cecotto was the winner of the 200-mile event.

Yamaha continued to build TZ750s right up until 1979, and in its final version (1977-on), it made 120bhp.

Make/Model: *Yamaha TZ750*

Engine type:
Liquid-cooled, inline-four two-stroke.
Displacement: *747cc (66.4 x 54mm)*
Fuel system: *4 x Mikuni VM34 carburettors*
Ignition: *capacitor discharge magneto*
Lubrication system: *two-stroke*
Maximum power: *105bhp @ 10,500rpm*
Maximum speed: *183mph/292km/h*

Transmission:
Gearbox: *6-speed*
Primary drive: *gears*
Clutch: *dry, multi-plate*
Final drive: *chain*

Chassis and Running Gear:
Frame type: *twin loop tubular steel*
Front suspension: *telescopic fork*
Rear suspension: *swingarm with twin shocks*
Front/rear wheels: *18in*
Front/rear tyres: *3.25/3.50*
Front brake: *2 x discs*
Rear brake: *single disc*
Weight: *157kg (dry)*
Fuel capacity: *29 litres*

Get the output sprocket more or less concentric with the swingarm pivot and chassis designers have half a chance of getting the handling right. It worked for Romero.

Yamaha TZ250C
1976 250cc

In 1968, the FIM began to implement new machine regulations for the world championships. To encourage more teams to take part, limits were put on the permitted number of cylinders and gears ratios. For example, from 1970 250cc engines were restricted to two cylinders and six speeds, while the limit for the 350cc and 500cc classes was four cylinders and six speeds.

Under the new rules, Yamaha's air-cooled piston-port two-stroke twins reigned supreme in the quarter-litre class and became numerically dominant in the 350cc series, too.

The Yamahas were sold ready to race and some riders enjoyed factory support. One was Finland's Jaarno Saarinen, who was given a water-cooled engine during 1972 and took that year's 250cc title. In the following season, Yamaha catalogued the TZ250 and TZ350 liquid-cooled twins.

TZ twins were fast and more reliable than their predecessors. Although they demanded a laborious and expensive maintenance regime, with new pistons and rebuilt crankshafts needed at frequent intervals, they were simple to work on. A privateer's dream come true, the TZ did much to bolster road racing from club to GP level through the seventies.

This is the only bike on which Tom Herron led a world championship. In 1976, after winning the Isle of Man TT he led Walter Villa - final champion - by one point.

This TZ250 is to 1976 specification, denoted by the C suffix. There were annual updates and the most visible on the C series were monoshock rear suspension and disc brakes. Ulsterman Tom Herron rode it to an Isle of Man Lightweight TT win and fourth place in the 1976 250cc world championship.

A colourful character who worked hard at his racing, Herron was equally at home on Grand Prix circuits and public roads courses. He organised his own international campaign in 1976, helped by his wife Andrea, mechanic Peter Kelly and two main sponsors, Rea Racing and bakery equipment manufacturer Jim Finlay.

At that year's TT, the last to hold GP status, Tom took his first Mountain Course in the 500cc Senior race on a TZ350, using a 251cc engine to make it eligible. The enlargement, carried out by many TZ350 riders, was usually done by increasing the stroke with offset crankpins since the hard-plated cylinder bores made boring-out impractical. Herron used German-made Hoeckle crankshafts.

Tom's 250cc TT win gave him a slender lead in the 250cc world series. He averaged a record 105.47mph for the 150 miles and was the first Irish rider to win two TTs in one year since Stanley Woods' 1935 Senior-Lightweight double. No doubt there were appropriate celebrations.

At the end of the season Herron was fourth in the 350cc world championship, as well holding that position in the quarter-litre class.

Herron got a place in the Suzuki GB team for 1979 but a high-speed crash at Northern Ireland's North West 200 meeting cost him his life.

The final TZ350 was the H series of 1981 but the TZ250 continued to be developed. There were major revisions for 1981 when separate cylinders replaced a single block and since 1991 a V-twin engine has been used.

1976 saw the appearance of the much awaited TZ250C, but the best news was the new monoshock chassis and disc brakes front and rear.

Revised porting, which included wider intake and transfer ports with altered angles of entry, raised compression and helped breathing through the carburettors.

Tucked away here is the monoshock for the rear suspension (bottom). Normal for most racing machines, a tachomoter and temperature guage is all that is needed (Top).

Specifications

Make/Model: *250cc Yamaha TZ250C*

Engine type:
Water-cooled, in-line twin piston-port two-stroke.
Displacement: *247cc (54 x 54mm)*
Ignition: *CDI magneto*
Fuel system: *petroil*
Lubrication system: *injected two-stroke plus premix*
Maximum power: *52ps @ 10,500rpm*
Maximum speed: *140mph/225km/h*

Transmission:
Gearbox: *6-speed*
Primary drive: *gears*
Clutch: *dry, multi-plate*
Final drive: *chain*

Chassis and Running Gear:
Frame type: *tubular double cradle*
Front suspension: *telescopic fork*
Rear suspension: *tubular swingarm, monoshock*
Front/rear wheels: *wire-spoked type 18in*
Front/rear tyres: *Dunlop RR96 3.00 x 18in/ KR1243.50 x 18in*
Front brake: *320mm disc*
Rear brake: *240mm disc*
Weight: *117kg (259lb)*
Fuel capacity: *n/a*

Yamaha YZR500 OW53
1981 500cc

The early eighties was a period of intense development for Yamaha's 500cc Grand Prix campaign. Kenny Roberts won the individual world championship three years running on YZR500s from 1978, 1979 and 1980 but the factory was under constant pressure from Suzuki, whose consistency had gained them the 500cc manufacturer's titles in the same years.

The piston port YZR500 in-line four had a very narrow power band, while Suzuki's square four disc valve engine was more tractable. To address this disadvantage, Yamaha devised its Power Valve, first used in the 1978 season. Controlled from the rev counter, the device used a mechanically operated shutter to lower the height of the exhaust port at reduced rpm. Less unburned mixture was allowed to escape from the combustion chamber, giving better torque in the lower rev range without affecting output at high rpm.

In 1980, OW48-coded factory YZR500s had a revised valve, with a guillotine shutter rather than the original rotating type. An aluminium frame made in square-section tube also appeared during the season, originally painted black to fool the opposition into thinking it was made of steel.

Midway through 1980 a revamped YZR500 engine was tried and proved vital in securing Robert's last 500cc title. The OW48R unit featured reversed outer cylinders, with near-straight exhaust pipes exiting from the tail fairing. This gave an instant power gain of 7ps, showing how sensitive a highly tuned two-stroke engine is to exhaust tuning. In some cases, the OW48R was raced with the old steel frame.

A rather worried looking Barry Sheene consults with mechanics at the 1980 Dutch Grand Prix.
Sheene left Suzuki for Yamaha in 1980 and was replace by Randy Mamola.

This machine is the subsequent 1981 OW53 type with the reversed cylinder engine in the tubular aluminium frame and was confirmed by Barry Sheene as the bike on which he came third in the 1981 Italian GP. After winning the 1976 and 1977 500cc world championships with Suzuki GB, Sheene left the team at the end of 1979 and set up his own equipe with American tuner Erv Kanemoto and sponsored by electronics brand Akai. Finding his non-factory Yamahas uncompetitive in 1980, he sought assistance from Japan and received increased support in 1981. Sheene was supplied with the OW53 early in the season, but was very put out when he saw that Roberts had a radically new and faster OW54 square four with disc valve induction. The British rider finished third in the Grand Prix des Nations at Monza on the in-line four and finally obtained one of the true 1981 bikes from Yamaha in mid-season. He won the final round of the year in Sweden, his last GP victory, as a major crash in practice for the 1982 British GP effectively ended his career as a grand prix contender.

Other riders who raced the final in-line YZR500 four were Holland's Boet Van Dulmen, who rode for the Europe-based Yamaha team, TT specialist Charlie Williams, who had access to factory machines for important 'real roads' events and leading UK short circuit star Steve Parrish, a friend of Sheene's who had also moved from Suzuki to Yamaha.

Specifications

Make/Model: *500cc Yamaha OW53*

Engine type:
Water-cooled, disc-valve two stroke, in-line four.
Displacement: *498cc (56 x 48.6mm)*
Fuel system: *4 x 38mm Mikuni carburettors*
Ignition: *CDI*
Lubrication system: *petroil mix*
Maximum power: *102ps @ 11,500rpm*
Maximum speed: *190mph/306km/h (dependent on gearing)*

Transmission:
Gearbox: *6-speed*
Primary drive: *gears*
Clutch: *dry, multi-plate*
Final drive: *chain*

Chassis and Running Gear:
Frame type: *aluminium tubular, double cradle*
Front suspension: *telescopic fork with anti-dive*
Rear suspension: *DeCarbon monoshock*
Front/rear wheels: *cast alloy 18in*
Front/rear tyres: *120/70 x 18in/170/60 x 18in*
Front brake: *2 x 280mm discs*
Rear brake: *220mm disc*
Weight: *130kg (287lb)*
Fuel capacity: *32 litres*

The 1981 OW53 specification machine was the successor to the OW48 R, and would be the last to mount a parallel four-cylinder engine.

The frame of the OW53 was a further development of the OW48s square, cross-section alluminium unit, which Kenny Roberts had tested the previous season.

1981 would see the introduction of the first square four engine (OW54) ridden by Kenny Roberts. In the meantime Sheene was lumbered with the OW53 for the start of the season.

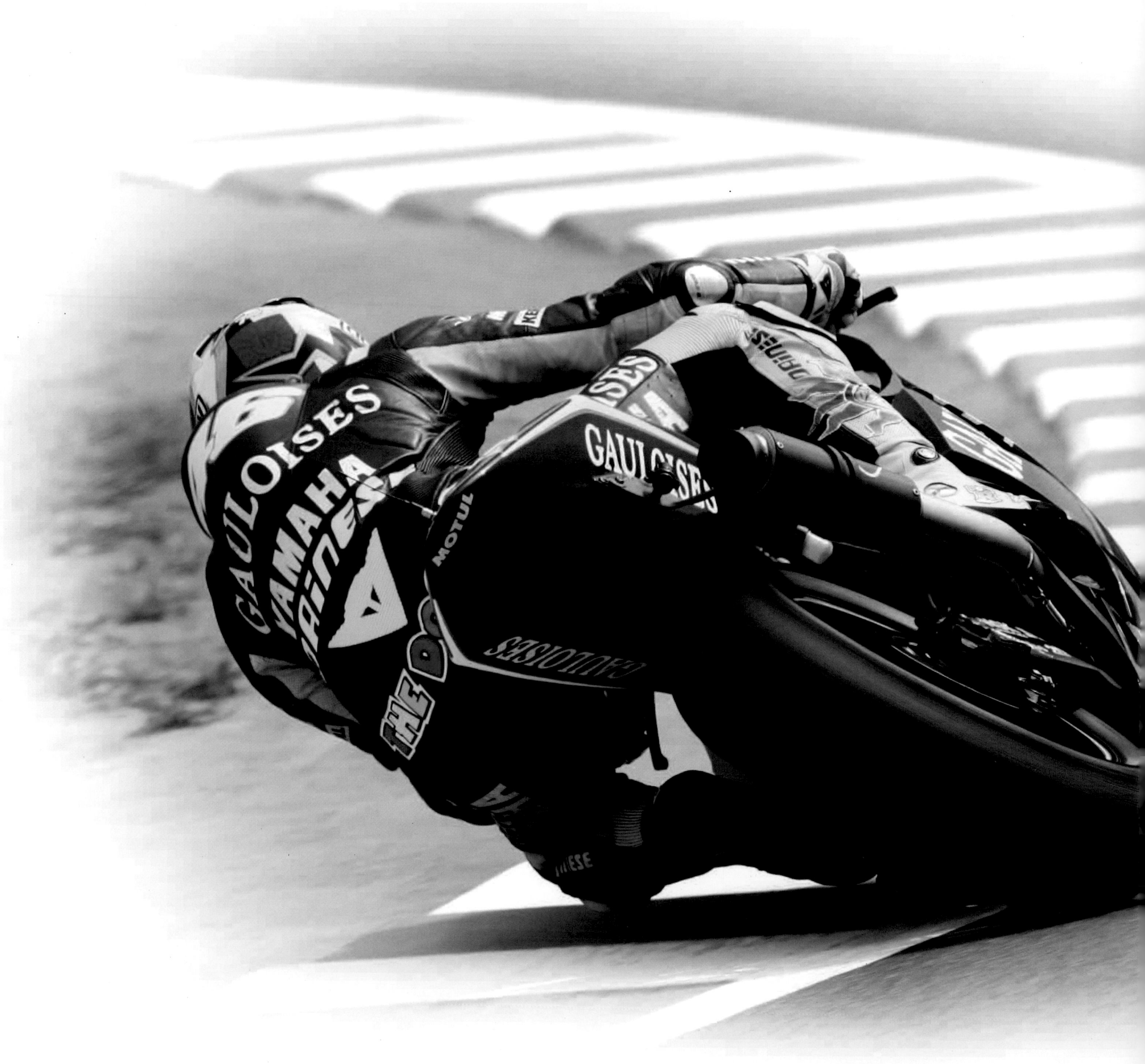
GAULOISES
YAMAHA
GAULOISES
MOTUL
GAULOISES

Yamaha M1 2004

M1 stands for Mission One and it would take three seasons and the very singular talents of Valentino Rossi before Yamaha could declare their mission accomplished.

Staying true to their road bike heritage, Yamaha's MotoGP offering is an across-the-frame four. For 2002 and 2003, the first two seasons of MotoGP, Yamaha stuck with the five-valve heads as found on their sportsbikes but abandoned their long-standing philosophy for the 2004 M1, conceding that a more conventional four-valve layout made for higher revs. They subsequently abandoned five-valve heads for the 2007 R1 superbike too. Where the 2003 990cc engine had made 230bhp at 14,500rpm, the 2004 motor made 235bhp at a higher rev ceiling of 15,500rpm. There was also a new irregularly spaced 'big-bang' firing order to give greater, torquier drive at lower revs and this would prove to be a Yamaha ace card on the exits of corners. Previously the M1 had a harsh two-stroke-like power delivery that the 2002 number one rider Max Biaggi constantly moaned about. However the new higher rev limit gave the camchains a hard time and they had to be changed frequently. For the 2005 season engine supremo Masao Furusawa would adopt gear-driven cams.

Yamaha's singularity is reflected in other details, sticking with road bike-style valve springs when Suzuki and now Kawasaki have opted for pneumatic valve closure. They also refused to go down the underseat pipe route, realising that there is no aerodynamic advantage in this approach and it can make it harder for the engineers to extract power.

View a man at the peak of his once-in-every-generation-or-three capabilities. Valentino Rossi is line perfect right up to the edge of the kerbing. Few have been able to work a turn like the maestro since the glory days of Mike Hailwood and Phil Read back in the so-called Golden Age of motorcycle GP racing. He has also done the previously believed to be impossible trick in the modern era of being world champ in three GP classes, 125, 250 and 500 then he made it four by adding MotoGP to his record. Phil Read was the only rider to have won in three classes prior to that.

But the key ingredient in Yamaha's 2004 success was the singularity of Italian ace Valentino Rossi, the first rider since the legendary Phil Read to win GP crowns in three capacity classes. Many had said that Read's feat would never be repeated because of the increased specialisation in each class. Rossi proved them wrong.

Critics of the world champ in 500GPs in 2001 and MotoGP in 2002 and 2003, all with Honda, had said he would be less dominant if he weren't riding for Honda.

Prior to the 2004 series, the close season rumour mill suggested that a disillusioned Rossi was poised to either switch to the World Rally Championship or sign to ride for Ducati in MotoGP, a prospect that sent Italian press and fans into a frenzy.

But Rossi set himself a far greater challenge and signed for Yamaha. With Biaggi and his other arch rival Sete Gibernau now on Honda RC211Vs, Rossi was not expected to retain his World Championship or even come close. Prior to Rossi signing for Yamaha the M1 had won only twice, in the hands of Biaggi in 2002.

Rossi confounded the critics by winning the season opener at Welkom in South Africa, once again propelling himself into the record books by becoming the first rider to win consecutive GPs riding for different manufacturers. A further eight wins that season gave him the title with 304 points to Gibernau's 257 and Biaggi's 217.

If Rossi looks pleased with himself he probably is, and with some justification. After years of Honda success he'd signed for the underdog Yamaha to rebut criticism that he only won through having the best bike. He shamed the competition in his previous Honda team and took the blue riband crown.

For 2004 the Yamaha back end worked well enough. For 2006 it presented sufficient 'chatter' problems to rule the M1 out of championship contention, handing the series to the consistent if lack-lustre Nicky Hayden, perhaps the most pedestrian champion since Kenny Roberts Jr in 2000.

Specifications

Make/Model: Yamaha M1

Engine type:
Liquid-cooled, in-line, 4-cylinder, 4-stroke DOHC
Displacement: 990cc (54.92cu in)
Fuel system: Fuel injection
Ignition system: Magnetti Marelli with adjustable mapping
Lubrication system: wet sump
Maximum power: 240ps plus
Maximum speed: 200mph (320kph) plus

Transmission:
Gearbox: 6-speed
Primary drive: gear
Clutch: dry, multi-plate
Final drive: chain

Chassis and Running Gear:
Frame type: Twin spar aluminium
Front suspension: Fully adjustable Ohlins inverted telescopic forks.
Rear suspension: Single Ohlins shock and rising-rate linkage.
Front/rear wheels: Marchesini 17in/16.5in (431.8mm/419.1mm)
Front/rear tyres: Michelin 17in/16.5in (431.8mm/419.1mm)
Front brake: Twin 320mm (12.59in) carbon disc with radial mounted 4-piston Brembo calipers.
Rear brake: Single 220mm (8.66in) ventilated stainless steel disc, with twin-piston Brembo calipers.
Weight: 148kg (326.28lbs)
Fuel capacity: 24Litres (5.27gal)

The Doctor, as his nickname goes, at it again (top). Side-mounted can is high and wide given prevailing MotoGP underseat pipe wisdom. Still seemed to work, however.

Superbike World Champions
FIM SBK/WSBK

Year	Rider	Manufacturer
2006	Troy BAYLISS (AUS)	Ducati 999F06
2005	Troy CORSER (AUS)	Suzuki GSXR1000K5
2004	James TOSELAND (GBR)	Ducati 999F04
2003	Neil HODGSON (GBR)	Ducati 999F03
2002	Colin EDWARDS (USA)	Honda VTR1000SP2
2001	Troy BAYLISS (AUS)	Ducati 996R
2000	Colin EDWARDS (USA)	Honda VTR1000SP1
1999	Carl FOGARTY (GBR)	Ducati 996
1998	Carl FOGARTY (GBR)	Ducati 996
1997	John KOCINSKI (USA)	Honda RC45
1996	Troy CORSER (AUS)	Ducati 916
1995	Carl FOGARTY (GBR)	Ducati 916
1994	Carl FOGARTY (GBR)	Ducati 916
1993	Scott RUSSELL (USA)	Kawasaki ZX7RR
1992	Doug POLEN (USA)	Ducati 888
1991	Doug POLEN (USA)	Ducati 888
1990	Raymond ROCHE (FRA)	Ducati 851
1989	Fred MERKEL (USA)	Honda RC30
1988	Fred MERKEL (USA)	Honda RC30

AMA Superbike Champions
(USA) /SBK

Year	Rider	Manufacturer
2006	Ben SPIES (USA)	Suzuki
2005	Matt MLADIN (AUS)	Suzuki
2004	Matt MLADIN (AUS)	Suzuki
2003	Matt MLADIN (AUS)	Suzuki
2002	Nicky HAYDEN (USA)	Honda
2001	Matt MLADIN (AUS)	Suzuki
2000	Matt MLADIN (AUS)	Suzuki
1999	Matt MLADIN (AUS)	Suzuki
1998	Ben BOSTROM (USA)	Honda
1997	Doug CHANDLER (USA)	Kawasaki
1996	Doug CHANDLER (USA)	Kawasaki
1995	Miguel DUHAMEL (CAN)	Honda
1994	Troy CORSER (AUS)	Ducati
1993	Doug POLEN (USA)	Ducati
1992	Scott RUSSELL (USA)	Kawasaki
1991	Thomas STEVENS (USA)	Yamaha
1990	Doug CHANDLER (USA)	Kawasaki
1989	Jamie JAMES (USA)	Suzuki
1988	Bubba SHOBERT (USA)	Honda
1987	Wayne RAINEY (USA)	Honda
1986	Fred MERKEL (USA)	Honda
1985	Fred MERKEL (USA)	Honda
1984	Fred MERKEL (USA)	Honda
1983	Wayne RAINEY (USA)	Kawasaki
1982	Eddie LAWSON (USA)	Kawasaki
1981	Eddie LAWSON (USA)	Kawasaki
1980	Wes COOLEY (USA)	Suzuki
1979	Wes COOLEY (USA)	Suzuki
1978	Reg PRIDMORE (GBR)	Kawasaki
1977	Reg PRIDMORE (GBR)	Kawasaki
1976	Reg PRIDMORE (GBR)	BMW

MotoGP and GP 500 World Champions/FIM Grand Prix/Moto GP1

Year	Rider	Manufacturer
2006	Nicky HAYDEN (USA)	Honda RC211V Moto GP (990cc)
2005	Valentino ROSSI (ITA)	Yamaha YZR-M1 Moto GP (990cc)
2004	Valentino ROSSI (ITA)	Yamaha YZR-M1 Moto GP (990cc)
2003	Valentino ROSSI (ITA)	Honda RC211V Moto GP (990cc)
2002	Valentino ROSSI (ITA)	Honda RC211V Moto GP (990cc)
2001	Valentino ROSSI (ITA)	Honda NSR500 GP 500
2000	Kenny ROBERTS Jr. (USA)	Suzuki RGV500 GP 500
1999	Alex CRIVILLE (SPA)	Honda NSR500 GP 500
1998	Mick DOOHAN (AUS)	Honda NSR500 GP 500
1997	Mick DOOHAN (AUS)	Honda NSR500 GP 500
1996	Mick DOOHAN (AUS)	Honda NSR500 GP 500
1995	Mick DOOHAN (AUS)	Honda NSR500 GP 500
1994	Mick DOOHAN (AUS)	Honda NSR500 GP 500
1993	Kevin SCHWANTZ (USA)	Suzuki RGV500 GP 500
1992	Wayne RAINEY (USA)	Yamaha YZR500 GP 500
1991	Wayne RAINEY (USA)	Yamaha YZR500 GP 500
1990	Wayne RAINEY (USA)	Yamaha YZR500 GP 500
1989	Eddie LAWSON (USA)	Honda NSR500 GP 500
1988	Eddie LAWSON (USA)	Yamaha YZR500 GP 500
1987	Wayne GARDNER (AUS)	Honda NSR500 GP 500
1986	Eddie LAWSON (USA)	Yamaha YZR500 GP 500
1985	Freddie SPENCER (USA)	Honda NSR500 GP 500
1984	Eddie LAWSON (USA)	Yamaha YZR500 GP 500
1983	Freddie SPENCER (USA)	Honda NS500 GP 500
1982	Franco UNCINI (ITA)	Suzuki RG500 GP 500
1981	Marco LUCCHINELLI (ITA)	Suzuki RG500 GP 500
1980	Kenny ROBERTS (USA)	Yamaha YZR500 GP 500
1979	Kenny ROBERTS (USA)	Yamaha YZR500 GP 500
1978	Kenny ROBERTS (USA)	Yamaha YZR500 GP 500

Year	Rider	Manufacturer
1977	Barry SHEENE (GBR)	Suzuki RG500 GP 500
1976	Barry SHEENE (GBR)	Suzuki RG500 GP 500
1975	Giacomo AGOSTINI (ITA)	Yamaha YZR500 GP 500
1974	Phil READ (GBR)	MV Agusta GP 500
1973	Phil READ (GBR)	MV Agusta GP 500
1972	Giacomo AGOSTINI (ITA)	MV Agusta GP 500
1971	Giacomo AGOSTINI (ITA)	MV Agusta GP 500
1970	Giacomo AGOSTINI (ITA)	MV Agusta GP 500
1969	Giacomo AGOSTINI (ITA)	MV Agusta GP 500
1968	Giacomo AGOSTINI (ITA)	MV Agusta GP 500
1967	Giacomo AGOSTINI (ITA)	MV Agusta GP 500
1966	Giacomo AGOSTINI (ITA)	MV Agusta GP 500
1965	Mike HAILWOOD (GBR)	MV Agusta GP 500
1964	Mike HAILWOOD (GBR)	MV Agusta GP 500
1963	Mike HAILWOOD (GBR)	MV Agusta GP 500
1962	Mike HAILWOOD (GBR)	MV Agusta GP 500
1961	Gary HOCKING (GBR)	MV Agusta GP 500
1960	John SURTEES (GBR)	MV Agusta GP 500
1959	John SURTEES (GBR)	MV Agusta GP 500
1958	John SURTEES (GBR)	MV Agusta GP 500
1957	Libero LIBERATI (ITA)	Gilera GP 500
1956	John SURTEES (GBR)	MV Agusta GP 500
1955	Geoff DUKE (GBR)	Gilera GP 500
1954	Geoff DUKE (GBR)	Gilera GP 500
1953	Geoff DUKE (GBR)	Gilera GP 500
1952	Umberto MASETTI (ITA)	Gilera GP 500
1951	Geoff DUKE (GBR)	Norton GP 500
1950	Umberto MASETTI (ITA)	Gilera GP 500
1949	Leslie GRAHAM (GBR)	AJS "Porcupine" GP 500

Supersport World Champions
FIM SS

Year	Rider	Manufacturer
2006	Sebastien CHARPENTIER (FRA)	Honda
2005	Sebastien CHARPENTIER (FRA)	Honda
2004	Karl MUGGERIDGE (AUS)	Honda
2003	Chris VERMEULEN (AUS)	Honda
2002	Fabien FORET (FRA)	Honda
2001	Andrew PITT (AUS)	Kawasaki
2000	Jorg TEUCHERT (GER)	Yamaha
1999	Stephane CHAMBON (FRA)	Suzuki
1998	Fabrizio PIROVANO (ITA)	Suzuki
1997	Paolo CASOLI (ITA)	Ducati

Isle of Man TT - Overall winners:

Wins	Rider
26	Joey Dunlop.
14	Mike Hailwood.
11	Steve Hislop, Dave Molyneux, Phillip McCallen, John McGuinness.
10	Giacomo Agostini, Rob Fisher, Stanley Woods.
9	Mick Boddice, David Jefferies, Siegfried Schauzu, Charlie Williams, Dave Saville.
8	Jim Moodie, Chas Mortimer, Phil Read.
7	Mick Grant, Tony Rutter, Ian Lougher.
6	Geoff Duke, Jimmie Guthrie, Jim Redman, John Surtees.
5	Robert Dunlop, Brian Read, Carlo Ubbiali, Alec Bennett, Bruce Anstey.
4	John Williams, Tarquinio Provini, Freddie Frith, Barry Smith, Dave Leach, Ray Pickrell, Bill Smith, Walter Handley, Klaus Enders, Jock Taylor, Trevor Ireson.
3	Adrian Archibald, Ian Simpson, Simon Beck, Carl Fogarty, Ray Amm, Luigi Taveri, Tom Herron, Bob McIntyre, Tony Jefferies, Alan Jackson jnr, Alex George, Dave Morris, Rob McElnea, Graeme Crosby, Harold Daniell, Phil Mellor, Barry Woodland, Barry Smith, Rolf Steinhausen, Walter Schneider, Max Deubel, Nick Crowe.
2	Ryan Farquhar, Shaun Harris, Iain Duffus, Chris Palmer, Charlie Collier, Cecil Sandford, Fergus Anderson, Hugh Anderson, Edwin Twemlow, Manliff Barrington, Kel Carruthers, Con Law, Eric Williams, Tom Sheard, Tim Hunt, Malcolm Uphill, Charlie J P Dodson, Howard R Davies, Bill Lomas, Eddie Laycock, Artie Bell, Gary Hocking, John Hartle, Jack A Porter, Trevor Nation, Fritz Hillebrand, Dick Greasley, Lowry Burton, Geoff Bell.
1	Michael Rutter, Nick Jefferies, Harry A Collier, Harry Reed, Jack Marshall, Rem Fowler, Cromie McCandless, R Les Graham, Steve Abbott, Dario Ambrosini, F A Applebee, Ken Arber, HR [Reg] Armstrong, Georg Auerbacher, Ross Williams, Peter Williams, Paul Williams, Cyril Williams, M Lockwood, Ken T Kavanagh, Ray Knight, Ewald Kluge, F A Applebee, Georg "Schorsch" Meier, Brian Morrison, Johnny Rea, Oliver Godfrey, H O [Tim] Wood, Frank Whiteway, Cyril G Pullin, Tommy C de la Hay, Fritz Scheidegger, Norman Brown, Trevor Burgess, Ralph Bryans, Roger Burnett, Jack Findlay, Phil Carpenter, Dave Croxford, Graham Penny, Ernst Degner, Mitsui Itoh, Stuart Graham, Ron Haslam, Bill Simpson, Martyn Sharpe, Keith Martin, Tony Rogers, Omobono Tenni, Florian Camathias.

Grand Prix motorcycle racing World Champions (1949-2006)

By Rider	
Rider	**Titles**
Giacomo Agostini	15 (500 cc: 8, 350 cc: 7)
Angel Nieto	13 (125 cc: 7, 50 cc: 6)
Mike Hailwood	9 (500 cc: 4, 350 cc: 2, 250 cc: 3)
Carlo Ubbiali	9 (250 cc: 3, 125 cc: 6)
Valentino Rossi	7 (MotoGP: 4, 500 cc: 1, 250 cc: 1, 125 cc: 1)
Phil Read	7 (500 cc: 2, 250 cc: 4, 125 cc: 1)
John Surtees	7 (500 cc: 4, 350 cc: 3)
Geoffrey Duke	6 (500 cc: 4, 350 cc: 2)
Jim Redman	6 (350 cc: 4, 250 cc: 2)
Michael Doohan	5 (500 cc: 5)
Anton Mang	5 (350 cc: 2, 250 cc: 3)
Hugh Anderson	4 (125 cc: 2, 50 cc: 2)
Kork Ballington	4 (350 cc: 2, 250 cc: 2)
Max Biaggi	4 (250 cc: 4)
Stefan Dörflinger	4 (80 cc: 2, 50 cc: 2)
Eddie Lawson	4 (500 cc: 4)
Jorge Martínez	4 (125 cc: 1, 80 cc: 3)
Walter Villa	4 (350 cc: 1, 250 cc: 3)

By Manufacturer (1949-2006)	500cc/ MotoGP	350cc	250cc	125cc	50/80cc	Total
Honda	17	6	19	15	2	59
MV Agusta	16	9	5	7		37
Yamaha	9	5	14	4		32
Suzuki	8			3	5	16
Aprilia			6	6		12
Kawasaki		4	4	1		9
Derbi				3	5	8
Kreidler					8	8
Moto Guzzi		3	3			6
Norton	3	2				5
Mondial			1	4		5
Garelli				4	1	5
Gilera	3	1				4
Minarelli				4		4
Bultaco					4	4
Morbidelli				3		3
Velocette		2				2
Benelli			2			2
Harley-Davidson			2			2
MBA				2		2
Krauser					2	2
AJS	1					1
Bimota - Yamaha		1				1
NSU			1			1
KTM				1		1
Zundapp					1	1
TOTALS	**57**	**33**	**57**	**57**	**28**	**232**

A

Agostini, Giacomo 45, 68, 88, 90, 92, 100, 140
Agusta, Corrado 86
Agusta, Count Domenico 86
AJS 7R3 10-13
Aldana, Dave 21
Alfieri, Giulio 79
Amm, Ray 12
Axtell, C R 36

B

Baker, Steve 140
Ballington, Kork 76
Battle of the Twins 15, 16
Bayliss, Troy 30
Beale, George 45
BEARS 15
Biaggi, Max 151, 152
Blair, Dr Gordon 97
Bol d'Or 80, 135
Bonera, Franco 92
Bradley, Rusty 68
Brelsford, Mark 36
Britten, John 15-16
Britten V1000 14-17
Bron, Rob 68
Brown, Bob 47
Bryans, Ralph 45
BSA 18-21
Rocket 18

C

Campbell, Keith 84
Carcano, Giulio 82
Carruthers, Kel 140
Castro, Don 21, 140
Cecotto, Johnny 140
Cereghini, Nico 80
Chili, Pierfrancesco 129
Coleman, Rod 12
Colnago, Giuseppe 84
Cooley, Wes 119
Cooper, John 97
Corser, Troy 28, 56
Crighton, Brian 104
Crosby, Graeme 111, 112, 119, 120
Croxford, Dave 100, 132

D

Dale, Dickie 84
Daytona 18, 21, 34, 68, 76, 97, 119, 120, 135, 140
Ditchburn, Barry 71, 72, 76
Ducati
888 27
916 26-9
999 30-3
Mike Hailwood Replica 24
NCR 22-5
DuHamel, Yvon 71, 76
Duke, Geoff 84
Dunlop, Joey 54, 59, 61, 107, 108, 120
Dunlop, Robert 61

E

Emde, Don 135
endurance races 79

F

Falappa, Giancarlo 28
Farmer, Mark 16
Farrant, Derek 12
Finlay, Jim 144
flat track racing 38
Fogarty, Carl 27, 28, 54, 56, 103
Fogarty, George 108
Fujiwara, Katsuaki 129
Furusawa, Masao 151

G

Gardner, Wayne 120
George, Alex 24, 132
Gibernau, Sete 152
Goddard, Peter 127, 129
Grant, Mick 71, 72, 76, 97, 100, 108, 119, 120, 132

H

Hailwood, Mike 18, 21, 22, 24, 45, 48, 72
Hansford, Gregg 72, 76
Harley-Davidson
KR 34, 38
XR flat tracker 38-41
XR-TT 34-7
XR750 38
Harris Performance Products 104, 123
Harris, Shaun 16
Harris, Steven 15
Hartog, Wil 111, 112, 116
Haslam, Ron 24, 52, 120
Hatch, H J 11
Hayden, Nicky 62, 65
Hele, Doug 18, 136
Hennen, Pat 116

Herron, Tom 116, 144
Hislop, Steve 54, 56, 103
Holden, Robert 16
Honda
CB750 21
NR500 51
NS500 50-3
RC30 27
RC45 27
RC160 47
RC161 47
RC162 46-9
RC164 43
RC165 43
RC166 45
RC174 42-5
RC211V 62-5
RS125 58-61
RVF750R RC45 56
VFR750R RC30 54-7

I

Imola 30, 86, 97
Irimajiri, Shoichiro 43
Isle of Man TT 16, 22, 24, 54, 59, 61, 68, 72, 103, 107-8, 112, 119, 120, 130, 132, 144

J

Jefferies, Nick 16
Jefferies, Tony 132
John Player Norton Monocoque 98-101
John Player Norton TX2 94-7
Johnson, Steve 76
Jolly, Steve 130

K

Kanemoto, Erv 148
Katayama, Takazumi 52
Kawasaki
H1-R 66-9
KR250 74-7
KR750 70-3
Kelly, Peter 144
Kitigawa, Keiichi 129

L

Laverda, Massimo 79
Laverda V6 78-81
Lawson, Eddie 76
Lawwill, Mert 34
Lomas, Bill 84
Lucchinelli, Marco 51, 111, 112

M

McCallen, Phillip 56, 103
McEwen, Jason 16
McIntyre, Bob 48
McLaughlin, Steve 140
McMenemy, Andy 59
Magni, Arturo 88, 90
Mamola, Randy 111, 112
Mang, Toni 76
Mann, Dick 21, 135
Marshall, Roger 119, 120
Maxton Engineering 104
Merkel, Fred 54
Middelburg, Jack 112
Miyakoshi, Shinichi 51
Molloy, Ginger 68, 75
Morrison, Brian 54
Mortimer, Chas 108
Moto Guzzi V8 82-5
MV Agusta
500 90-3
750 86-9

N

NCR (Nepoti and Caracchi Racing) 22
Newton, Ian 61
Nixon, Gary 21, 72
North, Rob 21
Norton
Commando 94
John Player Norton Monocoque 98-101
John Player Norton TX2 94-7
NRS588 102-5

O

O'Brien, Dick 34, 36

P

Pagani, Alberto 88
Parrish, Steve 115, 116, 148
Pasolini, Renzo 36, 92
Pedrosa, Dani 62
Perugini, Carlo 80
Phillis, Tom 47, 48
Pickrell, Ray 132
Pirovano, Fabrizio 28
Polen, Doug 28
Poole, Loren 16
Poore, Dennis 94

R

Rayborn, Carl 34, 36
Rea, John 107
Rea Racing 107, 144
Rea Yamaha 106-9
Read, Phil 22, 90, 92, 97, 108, 152
Redman, Jim 43
Repsol Honda RC211V 62-5
Roberts, Kenny 51, 52, 111, 123, 140, 147, 148
Romero, Gene 18, 21, 135, 136, 140
Rossi, Graziano 111
Rossi, Valentino 62, 65, 112, 151, 152
Russell, Scott 27, 28

S

Saarinen, Jaarno 90, 92, 142
Schlogl, Sepp 76
Scott, Hank 38
Scott, Jim 107
Scott, Mervyn 107
Sheene, Barry 51, 100, 111, 115, 116, 123, 125, 148
Simmonds, Dave 68, 72, 75
Slight, Aaron 28
Slippery Sam see Triumph T150 Trident
Smart, Paul 88, 97, 135
Smith, Bill 68
Spaggiari, Bruno 88
Spencer, Freddie 51, 52
Sports Motor Cycles 22
Sprayson, Ken 68
Springsteen, Jay 40
Stroud, Andrew 15
Superbike racing 27
Suzuki
GS1000 119
GSX-R750 WSB 126-9
XR14 92
XR22 115
XR23B 114-17
XR34 110-13
XR45 122-5
XR69-S/GS1000R 118-21
Swift, Fred 132
Symmons, Barry 104

T

Tait, Percy 88, 130, 132
Takahashi, Kunimitsu 48
Tamburini, Massimo 27
Tardozzi, Davide 28
Terblanche, Pierre 27
Triumph
750 triple 134-7
Trident 18
Trident T150 130-3

U

Uncini, Franco 125

V

Val Dulmen, Boet 148

W

Whitham, Jamie 28, 56, 127, 129
Williams, Charlie 148
Williams, Jack 12, 94
Williams, Les 132
Williams, Peter 94, 97, 99, 100
Williams, Ron 104
Woods, Stanley 144
Wynne, Steve 22

Y

Yamaha
M1 150-3
R1 151
TZ250C 142-5
TZ350 142, 144
TZ750 138-41
YZR500 90
YZR500 OW53 146-9
Yoshimura, 'Pops' 119

Z

Zen, Luciano 79
Zylstra, Peter 36

Acknowledgements

The Publisher and Authors would like to thank the following people and organisations for their kind help and input:

Bernie Saunders
Em Roberts
Jamie Whitham
John Wyatt
Nigel Everett
Steve Griffith
Ducati Museum, Bologna, Italy
Honda Europe
Yamaha Racing Team, Milan, Italy.

Mick Woollett photo archive, Hertfordshire, England
Mirco De Cet photography, Edgmond, England
Andrew Morland Photographic, Somerset, England.
AJRN Sports Photography - www.ajrn.com
Amulree Publications, Isle of Man.
Phil Masters Photography, Surrey, England.
Gold and Goose, London, England.

For supplying machines for photography:
Chris Wilson
Eddie Mateer
Robert McKendry
George Beale
The National Motorcycle Museum, Birmingham, England.
The National Motor Museum, Beaulieu, England
Moto Guzzi, Mandello del Lario, Italy.
Brian Slark at Barber Motorsport Museum, Birmingham, Alabama, USA.

Note from the Authors:
During its track career a racing motorcycle undergoes numerous modifications. Gearing, tyres, fuel systems and suspension are likely to be altered frequently. More radical work, such as frame and engine changes may be carried out as conditions demand. When machines are retired they may spend some time dismantled before being restored to rideable condition. For these reasons, it cannot be guaranteed that every machine featured here is exactly as it was when raced in anger.

Abbreviation used in this book:
FIM: Federation Internationale de Motorcyclisme - The world governing body of motorcycle sport
AMA: American Motorcyclists Association - The US governing body
ohc: overhead camshaft
dohc: double overhead camshafts
tohc: triple overhead camshafts
Power figures are given in PS (DIN standard). 1PS is equivalent to 0.986 brake horsepower (SAE? Standard), but the small difference is often discounted.